Praise 1

"A heartfelt guide to anyone see ~~~~~~~~~ their stones. You'll find practical ~~~~~~~~, ~~~~~~~~ ~~~~~~~, and unique correspondences to inspire your practice inside and out, all while you cultivate relationships with the spirits of the crystals themselves."
—**NICHOLAS PEARSON**, author of *Crystal Basics* and *Crystals for Psychic Self-Defense*

"*Spirit Crystals* isn't just about discovering the uses of crystals; it's about truly learning how to use them, something many crystal lovers with many shelves laden with colourful rocks are yearning to know. Jenny brilliantly guides readers through the journey of meeting their Spirit Crystal then leads you into extensive chapters unveiling deities, animals, plants, and divinatory skills that are waiting to greet you and align with you! This is more than a book—it's a crystal path you'll love getting lost down."
—**ADAM BARRALET**, author, YouTuber, podcaster, teacher, and Australia's very own rock star

"An innovative and experiential guide to working with six magical stones. Jenny's immersive meditations will unlock your soul connection to one of these crystal guides and its spiritual archetype. Deepen your connection with past life insights and wellness practices for personal growth and self-healing, all tailored to your personal Spirit Crystal. This gem of a book contains visualizations, rituals, spells, journal prompts, and mystic correspondences to support your path and crystal healing journey."
—**ETHAN LAZZERINI**, author of the Crystal Grids Power series

"Bell highlights the true significance of crystals, offering them the recognition they deserve. This book is perfect for anyone looking to deepen their connection with the crystal kingdom and seeking practical tools to bring its magic to life."
—**GEMMA PETHERBRIDGE**, author and founder of the Crystal Mystery School

"Have you ever found a crystal that just speaks to you? Maybe it is aesthetically pleasing, or when you touch it, the vibration feels amazing, and you can't understand why? Maybe you can sense that there is something about this crystal that connects you to a higher vibration. If so, you are ready for this book.... *Spirit Crystals* is such a unique book in that it not only connects you with crystals and helps you to understand their nature and attributes, but it also opens up a whole other dimension of connecting with crystals as guides, companions, and teachers.... Jenny C. Bell assists us in building a personal relationship with the crystals that we have come into contact with for our personal and collective development."

—**GRANDDAUGHTER CROW (A.K.A DR. JOY GRAY),** author of *Wisdom of the Natural World*

SPIRIT CRYSTALS

About the Author

Jenny C. Bell is a spiritual witch, creator, and founder of the inclusive, international, and online community Our Coven. For almost three decades, Jenny has practiced magic, fortune-telling, meditation, and crystal healing. Jenny is living her happily ever after in Southern Oregon with her husband, children, and pets. Learn more and connect with Jenny at jennycbell.com. TikTok: @jenny_c_bell Instagram: @ourcovencommunity

To Write to the Author

If you wish to contact the author or would like more information about this book, please write to the author in care of Llewellyn Worldwide Ltd. and we will forward your request. Both the author and the publisher appreciate hearing from you and learning of your enjoyment of this book and how it has helped you. Llewellyn Worldwide Ltd. cannot guarantee that every letter written to the author can be answered, but all will be forwarded. Please write to:

Jenny C. Bell
℅ Llewellyn Worldwide
2143 Wooddale Drive
Woodbury, MN 55125-2989
Please enclose a self-addressed stamped envelope for reply,
or $1.00 to cover costs. If outside the U.S.A., enclose
an international postal reply coupon.

Many of Llewellyn's authors have websites with additional information and resources. For more information, please visit our website at http://www.llewellyn .com.

SPIRIT CRYSTALS

Discover Your Crystal Guide for Healing and Empowerment

JENNY C. BELL

LLEWELLYN
WOODBURY, MINNESOTA

First Edition
First Printing, 2025

Book design by Christine Ha
Cover design by Kevin R. Brown
Interior illustrations by the Llewellyn Art Department

Llewellyn Publications is a registered trademark of Llewellyn Worldwide Ltd.

Library of Congress Cataloging-in-Publication Data (Pending)
ISBN: 978-0-7387-7905-8

Llewellyn Worldwide Ltd. does not participate in, endorse, or have any authority or responsibility concerning private business transactions between our authors and the public.

All mail addressed to the author is forwarded but the publisher cannot, unless specifically instructed by the author, give out an address or phone number.

Any internet references contained in this work are current at publication time, but the publisher cannot guarantee that a specific location will continue to be maintained. Please refer to the publisher's website for links to authors' websites and other sources.

Llewellyn Publications
A Division of Llewellyn Worldwide Ltd.
2143 Wooddale Drive
Woodbury, MN 55125-2989
www.llewellyn.com

Printed in the United States of America

*For Grandma Jane
and Grandpa Sal*

Disclaimer

This book contains information on crystals, herbs, yoga, meditation journeys, dance, and other aspects of a spiritual path. The author presents general advice that is not to be a substitute for the advice of a physician, psychiatrist, psychologist, or other professional. The information in this book is not intended to diagnose or treat any medical, mental, or emotional condition. The author and publisher advise readers that they have full responsibility for their safety and should know their limits. Always do your own research when using herbs and essential oils, and never leave a burning candle unattended. Making and drinking the tea suggested in this book is done at your own risk. Always see your health care provider before beginning a new health program including the use of teas, essential oils, herbs, and exercise. Journey meditation is done at your own risk and isn't a replacement for therapy. You are encouraged to consult a professional if you have any questions or concerns regarding any of the techniques in this book. Readers employing any methods or information from this book do so at their own risk, and the author and publisher accept no liability if adverse effects occur.

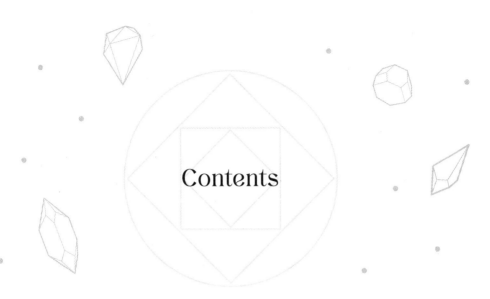

Contents

List of Practices

Introduction

Walking into a crystal shop is an entire vibe. There is the smell of herbs in the air, the glinting and gleaming of crystals and stones in a rainbow of colors. People often talk in hushed voices. It is like you have entered a sacred space or library. You can feel the possibilities all around you. There are cute handwritten signs that tell you what healing the crystals can bring to you. There is jewelry and carved crystals that are in the shape of angels, animals, and skulls. You spot a special collection of crystals under lock and key in a glass case. When you stand still and quiet, you can almost hear a buzzing and feel a vibration. You pick up a crystal and sense an excitement in your belly, a quickening of your heart, and a flush of energy in your whole body. Somehow you feel a connection to this stone that most people consider to be just a dead object resulting from the rock cycle you learned about in elementary school, but you know better. You sense there is more to crystals, and that's why you picked up this book.

This book is not here to be another A–Z reference of every crystal known. That has been done—and done a lot, I might add. Instead, in this book we are exploring something new and different. I am a psychic-channeler. This means that I connect to angels and Spirit Guides to receive information for myself and others. I recently received messages about Spirit Crystals. You know that you have a team of beings that help guide you during your incarnations. You may have even connected to some of this team in the form of your guardian angel or Spirit Guide. But what you may not have known but always sensed is that one of your guides is a crystal. This is why you are so drawn to crystals. They are your allies, your friends, and your healers, and one of them is your guide.

As you will learn in this book, crystals are full of life. Spirit Crystals belong to a special group of crystals, and they have come forward at this time to help heal and enlighten us. They are part of a high-vibrational soul group and want to connect to us and guide us. All crystals have energy, but Spirit Crystals are closer in energy to a Spirit Guide than other stones.

This book is a journey. We will begin by building a background for you on crystals that goes beyond geology. Then you will gain an understanding of how crystals like to be cared for. Next, you will go on a series of journeys to discover your Spirit Crystal. You may already have an inkling from flipping through this book or searching the table of contents, but I have to say that sometimes people are surprised by which crystal shows up to be their guide. Once you know your Spirit Crystal, you can jump into the corresponding chapter to gain a better understanding of yourself and the crystal while learning some healing techniques along the way. Even though you have one Spirit Crystal that you are deeply connected with, all the Spirit Crystals in this book are related and can be used together to offer tremendous healing. Finally, we will dive deeper into using Spirit Crystals in your life to create magic.

Throughout the book, you will see meditations, rituals, practices, spells, and journal questions. I encourage you to pause and try each one of these activities. They are here to amplify this book into more of a class than just a book to passively read.

Call the Quarters with the Spirit Crystals

I call upon the elementals and the elements of the south.
Great prasiolite, green and bright, help me discover the sage within.
I call upon the elementals and the elements of the west.
Mysterious smoky quartz, connect me to the rainbow bridge.
I call upon the elementals and the elements of the north.
Soft rose quartz, open my heart and help me receive.
I call upon the elementals and the elements of the east.
Quartz, give me the clarity to see beyond.
I call to Mother Earth beneath me, strong and deep.
Citrine, root me in the Great Mother so that I may never be alone.
I call to the cosmos above me, vast and wide.
Purple amethyst, open me to connect to the galactic wisdom.
And so it is!

PART ONE
Building Relationships

In these first few chapters, you will gain the background knowledge needed to discover and care for your Spirit Crystal. You will be given the information needed to select crystals, cleanse them, and care for them. You will also be given the encouragement and space to begin honing your intuition and start a meditation practice. The Spirit Crystals work best when they can communicate with you. This communication can only happen if you are open to receiving it. This openness can happen with the tools provided here. You will then be given the meditations and guidance to discover your own Spirit Crystal. Unlike astrology, your crystal isn't selected based off your birth date or other information. It is discovered through a soul calling. It calls to you. Are you ready to learn how to hear that call?

Chapter One
What Are the
Spirit Crystals?

Crystals are honored here. I see them as spiritual allies and friends. They are not to be used and tossed. They are living beings. When I see a crystal, I see and feel its life. Some people describe this experience as a buzzing or another sensation. In this chapter, you will gain an understanding of how a crystal is truly alive and how to become a caretaker to crystals. We cannot own a crystal because crystals are part of Mother Earth, and we belong to the earth, not the other way around. We are guardians and stewards of this earth, including crystals.

My childhood was spent exploring in the Mojave Desert. Rocks and stones weren't covered by grass or shaded by trees. They were everywhere and easy to collect and play with. I often collected quartz and stones to paint, make crafts with, or add to my mud pies. At nineteen, I was the treasurer of my geology club at college by day and by night a practicing witch. At the time, we had the cutest little crystal shop open in town, and I took my first course on crystals there. I received a stapled book by Dolfyn titled *Crystal Wisdom: Vol. VI* (still a great resource if you can find it) and pieces of tumbled clear quartz, aventurine, obsidian, rose quartz, carnelian, and hematite. Since this beginning, I have expanded my path to include using crystals in my Reiki healings, working with crystal skulls, and collecting out-of-print books on crystals.

In this book, I will impart my knowledge, but it's my hope that you will gain wisdom from your own connection and discoveries working with crystals. The best way to begin this journey of gaining wisdom, not just knowledge, is by opening to your intuition. Growth occurs when we let our knowledge meet our intuition, and this creates wisdom. My ability to be open to this wisdom is what led me to be here sharing Spirit Crystals with you.

Going into my Akashic Records is something I began after an impromptu past-life reading at a gem and mineral show in the Mojave Desert. Prior to this experience, I wasn't really interested in my past lives and felt no real desire to open the records. Every person has their own set of records in the Akasha, or ether. These records are the recordings of all your past lives as well as your future. We will dive deeper into how to open these records in chapter 7. This surprise reading, as well as many different people asking me about the records and assuming I knew what they were, led me to begin to enter the records to listen and receive information for myself and others. On February 24, 2022, I opened my Akashic Records and received this message:

> *You are on a mission to share about crystals.*
> *They will all be in the quartz family.*
> *Soul Crystals and Spirit Crystals only exist in the quartz family.*
> *The quartz is everlasting, it is ancient, it is not of this world,*
> *And that is the way someone can connect.*
> *They can connect soul to soul with the crystals*

The Spirit Crystals

Spirit Crystals are all in the quartz family. Clear quartz and any variation of it all belong to one Spirit Crystal consciousness. Whether or not it has a special name, like Lemurian seed, it's all the same. Clear quartz's archetype is the healer. A healer is a spiritual leader, and that is the role you have held in a past life and may be stepping into in this life again. Amethyst is for the alchemist, and this Spirit Crystal belongs to those who have lived a magical life in ancient Egypt. Citrine belongs to a group of people who are manifestors and have had a life in Atlantis. Smoky quartz is connected to those souls who can see beyond the veil and connect to loved ones who have already crossed the rainbow bridge into death. The rose quartzes all belong to those who are the lovers. These souls are like earth angels. Finally, prasiolite and aventurine belong to the great sages or wise people of this world and beyond.

The Archetypes

Reading the previous description, you may see yourself as some of these archetypes or none of them. Most people don't know intuitively which Spirit Crystal they are connected to. We are going to learn about crystals to prepare you for your connection to your Spirit Crystal. The truth is that we are all a little of each archetype. But the Spirit Crystal you connect with is the healing you need in this lifetime. This does mean that your Spirit Crystal can change from lifetime to lifetime. At some point, you may have connected to all of them, or you might have been with only one Spirit Crystal for all of your reincarnations.

The archetype that belongs to your Spirit Crystal may be thought of as the manifestation of your soul's mission here in this lifetime. This statement may feel heavy or intense but remember you have an entire life to live. Your spiritual journey is that of a spiral. The journey is not linear, and you will often circle back over the same lessons, evolving and healing a little more each time. The archetype that calls to you through your Spirit Crystal is a key to help you on your journey to being the best version of yourself.

One might see the archetype the medium and feel concerned. They may not feel safe with the dying or the dead. It may bring forward fears and images from scary movies. They may feel like now they have to drop everything and begin giving readings to grieving people. But it's important to remember that a soul mission or purpose doesn't have to be a career and that people often incarnate with more than one mission. Is it true that if you work with smoky quartz you can open yourself up to mediumship? Yes, but it doesn't mean you have to. It just means that you are being called to heal this part of yourself in this lifetime.

Crystals Are Alive!

A crystal is a special type of rock that is composed of minerals that are crystalline. This means that at an atomic level all the atoms are aligned in an orderly, repetitive formation. Crystals contain a sacred geometry within. They grow over thousands of years, usually beginning with a bit of water. You have probably seen white quartz rocks sold for landscaping. When you hold these rocks, you don't feel the same type of energy as you do with a crystal. This is because a crystal is quartz in its most pure form, without the addition of other minerals. Crystal quartz is composed of silicon and oxygen. Silicates are the most abundant minerals on the planet and almost all rocks have silicates within them. You have silica in your body and rely on oxygen to live, which means you and crystals share a similar ancestry. This connection through minerals and elements is why we are so drawn to crystals and why they can easily heal us.

Quartz is used in smartphones and other electronics because it can create electrical signals. Pure quartz has what is called a piezoelectric quality. It's a conduit, creator, and amplifier of energy but can also store, focus, and transform energy as well. I love when science catches up to spiritual beliefs. When it comes to quartz, there is scientific proof of its spiritual properties. Shamans have used quartz crystals to capture, amplify, and transmute energy for thousands of years. Tales from Atlantis speak of people using crystals beyond what science has imagined today. Many who remember their lives in Atlantis speak of crystals being used as power sources, not just conduits. These same people also claim crystals were used for healing and keeping people alive for hundreds of years.

Just because a stone isn't a crystal doesn't mean it doesn't have its own magic and healing abilities. All rocks and crystals are considered Stone People and are alive. You may have in your collection or have seen for sale a Lemurian seed crystal. A Lemurian seed is a type of clear quartz that holds records from the ancient land we now refer to as Lemuria, or Mu. But according to many Indigenous beliefs from North and South America, all stones are record keepers. Stone People hold, store, and transfer energy. Each one is a library of memories of both Mother Earth and those who live on Mother Earth. This may be why you find yourself picking up a stone on a walk along the beach or in a forest. You are drawn to the wisdom it holds.

All stones are holders of wisdom and offer potential healing, but what people have discovered over time is that pure crystals have a stronger type of magic. It's the purity of color, clarity, and shape that sets them apart from other stones. Crystals hold wisdom and records and offer magic, alchemy, and healing. They each connect to a larger collective unconsciousness, or collective soul. We, as humans, are connected to what's referred to as a collective unconsciousness, which some others call the quantum field. People often ask me how I can read cards or give Reiki to someone who isn't physically present with me. This is how I explain this connection. Once in meditation, I had a vision of myself standing in a spot with a glowing thread coming from my heart center. This thread extended beyond my body and connected me to a large glowing web. I could see that this web was connected to everyone on earth.

Crystals have a similar connection with one another. When you hold a piece of clear quartz crystal, you have the potential to not just connect with this piece of quartz in your hand but the collective consciousness of all the clear quartz on and within the earth. Connecting to this collective crystal soul allows you to receive deeper healing and insight beyond just connecting to the piece in your hand. Crystals are of a slower energy than other allies we connect with. A crystal changes and grows slowly in time, and when you connect with this energy, you will feel a slowing down. You will feel an immense calm.

Unlike some of your other Spirit Guides, your Spirit Crystal was never human. It hasn't been reincarnated and has always been mineral in origin. However, not all crystals are earthly in origin. We are made of stardust, as is our planet. When you connect with the collective soul of certain crystals, you may feel a connection to another planet, time, or place. This is because the crystals keep deep records for the universe, not just Mother Earth. They are Akashic recordkeepers of time and space.

Journal Pause

- What has been your experience with crystals so far?
- Do you feel connected to certain crystals. If so, which ones?
- Do you feel different when holding or wearing a crystal?
- Do you have an aversion to any type of crystal?
- Do you believe in past lives in places like Lemuria or Atlantis?
- Do you believe in past lives on other planets?

Choosing Crystals

Crystals are alive, but not everyone can sense this spirit—at least not right away. When choosing crystals, you might be able to trust your intuition and decide a crystal feels right and purchase it. But not everyone can sense this feeling or hold the crystal before purchasing, especially if they shop online. In this section, we will look at mundane and practical ways to choose crystals.

I know I live in a magical place because I can buy crystals at my local grocery store. I have also trick-or-treated for crystals. This kind man had crystals he was giving away instead of candy, and he let some mom friends and I have some. Not everyone lives in this kind of crystal-loving place. Chances are you might not have a store where you can buy crystals in person and need to rely on online shopping. I want you to know that online crystal shopping is perfectly fine as long as you avoid some of the scams out there, which you can easily do with the tips I provide here.

Ideally, you would pick out your crystals in person at a shop or in a mine or on Mother Earth. I have collected opal, granite, serpentine, and other treasures out in the field. Geologists and rock hounds love to share their knowledge, and information about places to collect crystals can be found in dusty old museum books or on no-frills blogs. A local museum might also have information about what rocks and minerals can be collected in your area. Gem and mineral shows that come to fairgrounds and parking lots are usually good places to shop too. There, you will often buy the crystal from the same person who found it. You can get a story and know that the crystal is not only the real deal but was collected in a kind way.

If you can visit a crystal shop or another shop that sells crystals, such as a botanica or metaphysical shop, that is a great opportunity as well. I will say, though, that sometimes depending on whom they source from, brick-and-mortar stores can sell fake or poor-quality crystals just like online stores. I recently went to one of my favorite places to buy crystals in my downtown. When I was ready to pay, the owner told me that he thought this batch of clear quartz might be glass made to look like quartz. He told me to just take the quartz I picked out for free because he didn't have a way of testing at the time. The crystals ended up being real, as there are a few things I always look for in quartz.

Something I like to keep in mind with all my purchases is that in a way we vote with our money. This is why when I first got engaged, I didn't want a diamond ring. Even before a popular movie was made, I knew about the atrocities committed in Africa to obtain many diamonds. Much later, we were able to find an ethically sourced diamond that I could proudly wear. When shopping for crystals online, I prefer independent sellers on Etsy or other small businesses. Yes, this may cost more than the big online conglomerate, but it's worth it to me. Read reviews, ask the seller questions, look at the photos, and know that if the "crystal" seems like it's at a really cheap price, it probably isn't a crystal.

It's perfectly fine to buy crystals secondhand. I encourage it. There are several social media groups for the rehoming of crystal skulls that include other crystals as well. Secondhand stores, estate sales, and yard sales are all fine to shop from too. In fact, you are more likely to get a crystal that needs a home and at a discount in this way. Since, you will learn how to cleanse a crystal you don't have to worry about the crystal storing anything negative. I have an aunt who would visit pawn shops to rescue pieces of turquoise. I am a thrifter and can often be found rescuing stones and crystals that feel sad to give them a happier spot in our home or on the land we reside.

PRACTICE
Ways to Test if a Crystal Is Real

The following is a list of different ways for you to determine whether your crystals are real. These tests are specifically for crystals in the quartz family but can often apply to other crystals and stones as well.

+ *Scratch test:* Using the Mohs hardness scale is one way for people to identify a mineral. A quartz is a 7 out of 10 on this scale, which makes it harder than glass. In fact, a steel nail is only at a 6.5. A quartz crystal will cut or etch a piece of glass. A simple test you can do at home to see if your quartz is real is getting a piece of glass and attempting to scratch it with your crystal. A cheap or thrifted picture frame is great for this purpose.

+ *Rainbows:* I like to buy crystals that contain rainbows. This rainbow means there is a prism effect that is usually caused by a natural imperfection in the crystal, such as a little crack. There are human-made iridescent effects placed on some crystals so that the whole thing shines like a rainbow. There is also a type of processing that uses modern science to create different types of "aura" crystals. Overall, there are many different methods to alter crystals and stones, and most often these processes involve extreme heat. Some people love these altered stones and find them to be powerful. I don't feel the same about these altered crystals, but please use your own intuition when deciding which crystals to add to your collection. The altered crystals are "real" but have been tampered with, and for me, it feels unnatural.

+ *Color:* Some crystals are heat-treated or dyed to obtain a darker or more vibrant color. Something to keep in mind is that true citrine's coloring is light and subtle. If the citrine being sold looks clustered like a piece of amethyst and resembles the color of an ice cube in root beer, it's not citrine but heat-treated amethyst from a lab. The same coloring trick can help you with rose quartz. Rose quartz is a subtle, soft baby pink, not a *Barbie* dark pink.

Crystal Size, Style, and Shape

You may have found me on social media saying that when it comes to crystals, size doesn't matter, which is true. A tiny chip of amethyst can connect to the same energy as one of those gorgeous amethyst-filled lava tubes that you can find me dreaming of and drooling over any time I see one. Size really doesn't matter. People prefer big crystals for the same reason they like fancy cars—they're great to look at and show off. So, if you have the budget for a big crystal, go for it! If you don't, you're not missing out. There is no correlation between the amount of healing energy and the size of the crystal. A tiny crystal can do the same amount of healing as a larger one.

For healing work with crystals, style also doesn't matter. A tumbled crystal and a raw crystal have the same healing abilities. For many, it just comes down to preference. If you want to carry or sleep with your crystals, you probably want them tumbled. If you want to use your crystals in candles, spell bottles, or other witchy work, you may want crystal beads or chipped crystals, which you can buy in little glass jars.

As far as shapes are concerned, when a crystal is carved into a bowl, animal, skull, or other shape, this alters the crystal's energy—especially in the case of a skull. The crystal is now not only connected to its crystal soul family but also the symbolism in our collective consciousness of the shape. A crystal skull, whether it be human, alien, or dragon, is inviting a guide to use it as a vessel to work with and connect with others. For our work with Spirit Crystals, I prefer raw, naturally shaped (not tumbled) crystals and skulls. These two have the greatest potential for connection and are easiest to work with. But please use your intuition and be mindful of your budget and preference.

Cleansing and Cleaning Crystals

Crystals pick up energy just like you do, and crystals need more than just a moon bath to be cleansed. The term *cleaning* is what it sounds like—the physical cleaning of mud or dust from a crystal. *Cleansing* is a spiritual term that means to remove unwanted energies. Some people wonder why we need to cleanse something that is natural, but what we have to remember is that the crystal was taken from its natural place and touched a lot of hands before it reached you. Sometimes the mining can be traumatic for a crystal. I visited a boron mining site once and saw a part of a mountain blown up. It wasn't a natural explosion like that of a volcano. It was jarring. Then there are all the people who handle the crystal before you even pick it up. People can be unhappy or angry, and crystals can pick up this energy. With the exception of selenite, all crystals need cleansing. Selenite is self-cleansing in part because it sheds little splinters. It is considered one of the few crystals that never needs cleansing. I keep a large piece in my living area. It picks up all kinds of energy but always feels balanced.

PRACTICE
How to Cleanse Crystals

The following ways to cleanse crystals are great for when you first purchase your crystals, after you use them for heavy healing, or when you just feel they need it.

- *Castile soap:* Most crystals and stones that don't end in *-ite* can be cleaned with soap and water. Selenite, halite, calcite, and other *-ites* don't do well in water. Gypsum is another stone that cannot be washed with water. Please do some research before submerging any of your crystals or stones in water. If you are unsure whether you can put your crystal in water, consider the following: Is it tumbled? Tumbling means the crystal was in a tumbler with grit and water for days, so it can definitely be in water. Does the crystal crumble or flake? If so, don't put it in water. A note that this isn't a cleansing step but more of a cleaning step. This is a way to get your crystal free of any dust or grime.

+ *Sunshine:* Putting a crystal in sunshine is the best way to cleanse it. Indirect sun is best, so place your crystals in the shade outside on a sunny day. After I wash a crystal, I usually set out a towel or blanket on the grass and set it in the sun for about an hour. I say something like "Thank you, Father Sun and Mother Earth, for cleansing these crystals, releasing any energy that is no longer serving them. Blessed be." There are some crystals that will fade in the sun, such as fluorite, but most do just fine.

+ *Sacred smoke:* If you have a crystal that cannot be in the sun or want to do a quicker cleanse after you've used the crystal in a grid or for some healing, you can pass the crystal through sacred smoke. Smudging with white sage is a closed practice and isn't recommended unless this practice belongs to your culture. Both white sage and palo santo are under threat of being endangered. Alternatives to these plants include dried mugwort, bay leaves, rosemary, culinary sage, cedar bark, or a high-quality incense. Light your chosen herb or incense and pass your crystal through the smoke while saying something like "Thank you to (name of the herb) and the element of air for cleansing this crystal of any and all impurities, letting them go up in smoke. Blessed be."

+ *Selenite:* Not only is selenite self-cleansing but it will also cleanse other crystals for you! It's inexpensive, too, which is a bonus. You can buy bowls or slabs of selenite to rest your crystals on for a quick cleanse. You can also pass a selenite wand over your crystals to cleanse them. Selenite is connected to the moon, so this cleansing is even better to perform at night while calling on the aid of your favorite moon deity. "Thank you, Diana, for cleansing this crystal of anything that doesn't belong to it, releasing old stuck energies with the help of this selenite. Blessed be."

+ *Dirt*: When a crystal has picked up a lot of heavy energy, whether it be from healing, spellwork, or just from being around low-vibe people, it may need some time in Mother Earth. In this case, you can bury the crystal in a potted plant or in your garden for a full moon cycle—new moon to full moon. After the cycle, unbury your crystal. Thank Mother Earth and give the crystal a washing and some sunshine. While burying you can say, "Thank you, Mother Earth, for returning this crystal to your womb. May it release all that it has picked up and be free once again. Thank you, Mother, for recycling this negativity as fertilizer. Blessed be."

+ *Fire*: This method isn't for everyone, and I recommend doing this with caution. If you feel a crystal has come in contact with a really intense negative energy, light a candle and pass the crystal through the flame several times. You can use some kitchen tongs or a similar tool to hold the crystal. Don't leave it in the fire; just pass it through three times, saying something like "I call on the element of fire and Archangel Michael for burning away any dark entities or energies that are held by this crystal. May they burn in the fire. May this crystal be free. Amen." Now, this isn't something most people ever have to do, but depending on whom you use your crystals to heal, you may feel you need this someday.

+ *Energy healing*: If you are comfortable with and trained in energy healing, such as Reiki, you can use this method to cleanse your crystals. I am a Reiki master and still prefer the washing and sun methods for new purchases. But in between uses and healings, I feel Reiki does a great job of cleansing the crystals. Simply hold the crystals in your hands and give them healing just as you would do for a client.

Storing Crystals

Crystals are happiest when they are out in the light and kept dust free. I have crystals all around my home, and every once in a while, I gather them all and give them a rinse and an hour in the sunshine. When I am not using a crystal as part of a grid or for healing, I keep it with others in a natural bowl. You can find beautiful bowls made of selenite, fluorite, soapstone, and wood. Keep crystals away from plastic and out of dark bags that hide them from the light. If you must keep them in a drawer or tucked away, make sure to give them some sun before working with them.

Readying Yourself to Meet Your Spirit Crystal

You now have a better understanding of how to choose, cleanse, and store crystals. This knowledge will be useful later when you decide to purchase your Spirit Crystal or other stone allies. This knowledge is one half of connecting to your Spirit Crystal. The other half is readying yourself. You will be guided to retrieve your Spirit Crystal, which means you need to have a level of openness to do so. The best way to prepare yourself for further practices in this book are to begin to listen to your intuition.

PRACTICE
Opening to Intuition

Intuition is your greatest gift. The truth is you have intuition and always have. Everyone is born with it, but we live in a time when most cultures and societies encourage the logical mind over the intuitive heart. In order to encourage your intuition to become stronger, you have to reclaim it and unlearn some societal rules working against it. Here are some tips to help you to open to intuition again. Pick at least one exercise to try for a week or two.

+ *Keep a dream journal.* Even if your dreams make little sense to you, keeping a journal will help you notice repeating symbols or patterns. Our unconscious is where our intuition lives, and our dreams live there as well.

+ *Look for repeating messages in the world around you.* If you are seeing the same number all the time or maybe the same animal, there is an intuitive message for you to unfold. It may be that you seem to look at the clock at the same time every day. Research that number. It may be that the same animal keeps coming to you in person, in dreams, or while scrolling. Look to see what message that animal holds.

+ *Pay attention to what your body is telling you.* Does your heart race at a certain thought or idea? Ask why. Do you suddenly get butterflies in your stomach? Ask why. Our bodies are in constant communication with us.

+ *Meditate.* Even if you just sit with your thoughts racing for five minutes every day, you will begin to invite your intuition back into your life. You are providing space for it to communicate with you.

+ *Get outside more.* Sit or walk in silence in nature whenever you can. Let your thoughts go and just take notice. What is the temperature? What colors do you see? What do you smell? Get back into your body and out of your head.

+ *Pick up an oracle or tarot deck.* Pull a card every day and decide what it means for you without looking up the author's message in the book.

Starting a Meditation Practice

Intuition begins to open you to listening to your own guidance. Meditation furthers this practice. If you are someone who is new to meditation or doesn't enjoy meditation, I understand. Remember that meditation is a practice. I have been meditating for over two decades, and I still have times of struggle. If you are already someone who is very comfortable with meditation, you may not need these tips, but I ask you to humbly take on a beginner's mind. See the information shared with fresh eyes, and you might just remember some basics that have been lost over the course of your practice. The following list has some basic tips I have gathered over my years of practicing and teaching meditation.

+ *Begin with learning how to take deep, slow breaths.* Put your hands on your belly, fill it slowly with air, then slowly release it. I call this balloon breath. You can practice this three to five times a day before you even "officially" try a meditation. In fact, any time you focus on your breathing, it really is a meditation. Deep breathing takes the automation of breathing and makes it conscious. This shift helps the mind tune into the body and its needs. This breath can be both relaxing and grounding. Deep breathing calms your nervous system, and for many of us, our nervous systems are in a constant state of stress.

+ *Practice being in the present moment.* Take a deep breath and try to just be here right now—as in not thinking about the future or what happened in the past. This practice can be achieved through some verbal or in-your-head narration. For example, when you are standing and washing dishes at the sink and your mind begins to get into a loop or is working on a problem, say aloud or in your head, "I am washing this dish. The water is warm. The soap smells like lavender. I am scrubbing with a blue sponge." This narration forces you back to the present moment and clears the mind of the loop it was in.

+ *Practice observing your thoughts.* Take a moment to just observe your thoughts as if they are happening to someone else. This practice can be tricky, but it will benefit you in your meditation practice. It creates a huge shift in your life. You are no longer your thoughts or emotions but the soul observing them. We can easily think we are our thoughts or our feelings, but really those are ego and bodily occurrences. You are neither your ego nor your body but that soul observing it all. When you observe your thoughts, you are not judging them but simply noticing them. For example, your inner dialogue may sound like this: "I am thinking about how embarrassed I was at what I said to that woman at the grocery store. I am feeling ashamed now even though it happened yesterday."

+ *If you can, have a set place to meditate.* Having a specific place will help establish a routine. Some people like to use an essential oil or an incense to add to the routine, but it is not necessary. Smell does help us connect to memory and that helps create routines. Your meditation spot doesn't have to be anything fancy, just a place you feel comfortable. The same place and scent develop a routine and pattern for your unconscious mind and makes maintaining a practice easier. For those in a small space, this can be as simple as a cushion tucked under your bed. You can sit on the same cushion every day, placing it by the same window.

+ *Try to be comfortable while you meditate.* You can sit, walk, stand, or lie down. You may use a chair or a bed. I prefer to meditate after yoga, and you may also look for a time when your body feels its best. This time may be after exercise, sleep, or bathing, but again, it is not necessary. If you are a hyperactive person, after exercise may be the best time for you, and you don't have to be still during your meditation. You can use fidgets (prayer beads), you can roll a tennis ball under your foot while in a chair, or you can pace and walk around.

+ *Try not to worry whether you are doing it right; rephrase that question into "Am I trying? Am I being here now?"* If the answer is yes, then yes, you are doing it right. So many people will ask me if they are doing the meditation right or how they can know if they are doing it right. The answer is that if you tried, you did it right. Some days you may feel like a reincarnated monk and can just meditate so easily, and other times you might feel like a distracted child trying to still your mind. It is all right.

+ *Be kind to yourself.* Don't get upset if you forget to practice or you just can't focus. Each day is a new day. Each moment, you are new. Let mistakes go and try again. In the case of meditation, practice doesn't make perfect. Practice makes it a routine. This routine helps establish true self-care and an opportunity to heal.

Divergence and Meditation

I am neurodivergent. I fully embrace my divergence because I feel it's a gift more than a problem or something I need to fix. I have empathy for anyone with a divergence who doesn't feel the typical guided meditation format was meant for them. I want to take a moment to give alternatives for people who have a hard time with neurotypical mediation formats.

+ *Visualizing:* For those with aphantasia or other blocks to visualization when a meditation guide suggests you visualize or imagine, try to feel or sense instead. Feel the connection in your body. Notice tingling, ringing in your ears, or other sensations that let you know you are experiencing something different. We use image-filled journeying in meditation as a way to help people leave the mundane 3D world behind and step into the invisible. But for you, it will be more of a shift in feeling than in seeing. For example, when you are guided to walk among trees—feel what it is like to do this instead.

+ *Stillness:* If you have trouble sitting still, by all means move around, walk, or fidget with your crystal(s) while you meditate. You can easily record meditations and pace as you listen. You can hold a fidget toy in your hands or roll tennis balls under your feet.

+ *Don't want to close your eyes:* If you don't like to close your eyes, then don't. Stare at your crystal with your eyes relaxed and out of focus instead. This is called drishti in yoga. It's a practice that focuses your gaze, and there are a ton of videos that can show you just how to do this.

+ *Slower to process or remember:* If you want guidance at your own pace, you can record yourself reading the meditations in this book or ask a friend or loved one to read them to you. Feel free to practice a single meditation over and over again until you feel that you have completed it the way you would like.

+ *Don't like silence:* Silence is not for everyone. There is a lot of free meditation music available. I love drumming and find it helps me journey deeper in meditation. Look into singing bowls, hertz frequencies, and the sound of flutes, ocean waves, or anything else you might enjoy.

MEDITATION
Five-Minute Sit

The following meditation is a practice, as are all meditations. I want you to try this meditation with all the suggestions and accommodations from this chapter in mind. It's important for you to find a way that meditation works for you at this time. Just because ten years ago you enjoyed mantra meditation at a retreat doesn't mean that same technique will feel good to you now. We are constantly evolving and shifting. On this spiritual journey, we need different healing at different times for different reasons. Don't keep yourself in a box. Experiment and explore.

You may want to walk during this practice, sit, or lie comfortably. The key is to allow your body to be as comfortable as it can so it doesn't distract you. If thoughts pop up during this practice, allow yourself to notice them and then let them go. Once you are comfortable, set a timer for five minutes. Then to your best ability, focus on your breath. You might want to say in your mind "in and out" or "up and down" for each breath movement. Or you might want to count your breaths. With each breath, begin again. Each breath offers you a moment of meditation. See if you can be still. See if you can quiet your thoughts. This five-minute moment is just a time to explore and observe.

Journal Pause

- How did this five-minute meditation feel?
- What did you observe about your body?
- What did you observe about your mind?
- What would you do differently next time?

There Is No Spirit Without You

We are not just exploring crystals in this book, but ourselves. Spirit Crystals offer guidance and healing but only if you are able to listen. Meditation and intuition are both forms of listening. Allow yourself the time, space, and energy to listen. Don't be concerned with a rigid practice or whether you are "doing it right." Instead, allow yourself the time and space to explore. Build in time in your day to check in with your own wisdom. Tap into your own breathing and let your mind clear. Ask yourself what you need to know at this time or what your own heart is trying to tell you. Give yourself the time to receive and wisdom will come.

Chapter Two
Laying Out the Groundwork

Y ou are the magic. You are the medicine and the conduit. The crystals are your allies, friends, and helpers, but they only work when you are open to connection. You must do the healing, walk the path, and learn how to open yourself up to this connection. We are all capable of such a spiritual connection—no matter how long we have been on this path. We just have to be open and willing to receive. Reception is an aspect of the divine feminine. The divine feminine, or goddess energy, resides in all of us regardless of gender. We are all both masculine and feminine. When we are looking to connect spiritually with a crystal, we are working in our divine feminine energy. This energy is enhanced and strengthened when we participate in practices such as meditation, journaling, and reflection. In this chapter, there will be exercises that help you to be in your feminine energy to ready you for connection to your Spirit Crystal.

My Story on Connection

I once had a vision of a past life where I created this huge crystal grid and buried a life-size clear quartz crystal skull in the middle. I have always loved skulls. I think they're beautiful, and they offer me a peace that I can never really explain to others. I don't see a morbid representation of death but a celebration of life. After this meditation, I went on Etsy and found tiny Lemurian quartz crystal skulls for sale. Tum-ma (but sounds closer to "Tommy"), my Lemurian quartz skull, came in the mail, and I really fell in love. Tommy—with the help of another

Lemurian quartz skull, named Alana—guided me on how to teach others to connect with and activate crystals. For those interested in working with skulls, we will have a more in-depth look at crystal skulls in the last chapter.

The skulls taught me how to connect with a crystal. Prior to this, I always loved collecting crystals but never knew how to listen to and learn from them. Since then, I have gone on to teach hundreds of people how to intuitively connect with crystals. This connection has freed people from using reference books and websites to look up the meaning of a crystal. Instead, they rely on their own connections. And so will you. Connecting with crystals is the best way to discover your Spirit Crystal. But my connection method will also allow you to activate and connect with any crystal, stone, seashell, or even plant or animal. The way that we make crystals our allies and forge a connection is meditation, which is the key to developing your spiritual self.

Crystals and Chakras

Each of the Spirit Crystals is associated with certain chakras. Your chakras are where all your magic manifests from. This rainbow body of light is important to understand and connect with when it comes to working with your crystals. The Spirit Crystals naturally connect to your chakras, and this is how healing takes place. Before anything else, let's start with a meditation to gain some insight into your own chakras.

MEDITATION
Rainbow Breathing Meditation

For this meditation, decide whether you'd like your eyes closed or open and how to position your body. Decide what time to practice and where to do so. Also give thought to whether you want to record yourself speaking the instructions or just read them a few times and do it from memory.

For the next series of breaths, you will practice visualization and/or sensation in your body. This meditation is aimed toward you understanding how your body connects and works in meditation. You will breathe in a series of colors. Make your breathing slow and purposeful. Slowly inhale to fill up your belly and chest and slowly exhale. You may hold the breath a bit before exhaling or not; the choice is yours. You may also decide whether to breathe in and out through your nose or maybe in through your nose and out through your mouth.

Get comfortable, close your eyes (or not), take a deep breath, then sigh it out. Now on your next deep breath, visualize or feel that you are breathing in the color red. You decide the shade of red and how it appears to you. See the red entering your body and leaving as you exhale. Stay with the color red until you feel you have a grasp of what it looks or feels like for you.

Next, breathe in and out the color orange. What shade is this orange? What does orange feel like? Where does orange go in your body? Stay with orange until you get a sense of it.

Then move on to breathing in the color yellow, working on the same concentration as you did with the first two colors. If thoughts arise, simply observe them and let them go, then return to focusing on the color. It might help you to use the name of the color like a mantra aloud or in your head, saying, "Yellow, yellow, yellow…"

Next, introduce the color green, and stay with it until you feel satisfied. Then move to a turquoise blue. Next move to a deep indigo blue. Finally breathe in and out a light purple or violet color.

Once you have gone through all the colors, release them, open your eyes, and journal about your experience before moving on. I do want to share that my daughter Lucy invented this meditation for us, and it's a great one for people of all ages.

Journal Pause

- How did this meditation feel?
- Which color(s) were the easiest to connect with?
- Which color(s) were the hardest to connect with?

If this meditation didn't go well for you, try it again. Change up the experience by choosing a different time of day, body position, or background music or by employing some incense or a candle to set the mood. This meditation is intended to help you connect with your chakras. Each of these rainbow colors is connected to one of your chakras. You can use this breathing meditation to determine which chakras are in need of healing (the colors you struggle connecting with).

Chakras for Crystal Connection

I have been studying and connecting with chakras for years. The chakra system is complex yet simple. The chakras are not something we heal and move on from. They are constantly shifting and changing and provide a lifelong journey of exploration. Sometimes they are all spinning and bright. Other times one or more is imbalanced. Crystals help bring balance to our chakras. Crystal energy is subtle and will not cause a sudden awakening or massive shift in our energy system. This is one reason why crystals are great for chakra balancing.

+ *Root chakra:* Associated with the coccyx and the color red, this chakra is your place of safety. When this chakra is functioning well, you have a sense of being safe in your body and surroundings as well as being grounded. When this chakra is not healthy, there are issues with money, shopping, anxiety, and fear. Crystals to help heal and balance this chakra are obsidian, onyx, citrine, garnet, and red jasper. A clear quartz works with the healing and balancing of any chakra.

+ *Sacral chakra:* The sacral chakra is associated with your sexual organs and the color orange. When this chakra is healthy, you're in your creative state and ideas flow easily through you. This is the energetic womb of your chakra system. When it's functioning well, you feel safe to create the life you desire and can be in joy. When this chakra is unhealthy, there are issues with addictions and overeating and an imbalance in sexuality. Crystals to help heal and balance this chakra are moonstone, smoky quartz, carnelian, and kunzite. Some people might look at this list of crystals and feel that these choices are not traditional. This is because these are the crystals I have found in my own practice to help balance this chakra. I encourage you to use your own intuition as well. The sacral chakra is a womb, and therefore, crystals that have a feminine energy are very healing for us regardless of gender.

+ *Solar plexus chakra:* This chakra is associated with the color yellow and your solar plexus (between your belly button and ribs). When this chakra is healthy, you feel empowered and use this power in a positive way. When it's unhealthy, you may feel afraid to make changes in your life, limited and trapped by your ego. The ego likes to distort power or create the dichotomy of victim or villain. Crystals that help the health of your solar plexus are topaz, sunstone, citrine, and tiger's eye.

+ *Heart chakra:* Associated with your heart space, which is the middle of your chest, your heart, and the colors green and pink, the heart chakra, when healthy, allows you to give and receive love in balance. This chakra is what really opens you up to spiritual awakenings and experiences. If the upper three chakras are open but the heart is closed, you will act holier than thou and have a cold approach to magic and spirituality. If your lower three chakras are functioning but the heart is closed, you will have a hard time opening to channeling or divine input. When this chakra is unhealthy, you may feel unworthy, unloved, or incomplete. Crystals for heart chakra healing are rose quartz, watermelon tourmaline, and kunzite.

+ *Throat chakra:* Associated with your throat, voice, mouth, thyroid, middle of collar bones, and the color blue, the throat chakra, when healthy, allows you to speak your truth and know your own voice. Many people on a spiritual path have to work to heal and open their throat chakra. In our current Western patriarchal society, many carry wounds of feeling strange or alien for having spiritual gifts. Fear of persecution from this life or a past life may linger. When this chakra is unhealthy, you may feel that no one understands you or cares to listen to you. You may be afraid to share your truth. The best crystals for your throat chakra are turquoise, blue tiger's eye, labradorite, prasiolite, aventurine, and lapis lazuli.

+ *Third eye chakra:* Associated with the color indigo and the center between your eyebrows and eyes, the third eye chakra, when in balance, gives you clarity of mind, allows you to imagine, and opens you up to divine input. This is your psychic chakra and allows you to see the future and dream. Even if you cannot envision or imagine in your mind's eye, the third eye chakra can manifest in other ways of "seeing," such as an inner knowing, hearing, or feeling. When this chakra is unhealthy, you may be afraid to see your future and blinded toward truths. The crystals that work best with healing and opening your third eye are clear quartz, Lemurian seeds, and moldavite.

+ *Crown chakra:* This chakra is associated with the top of your head and beyond as well as the colors violet and white. When your crown chakra is healthy and open, you are opened to Creator energy and can become a clear channel. You feel connected and spiritual. This is the chakra that allows divine input to go into your body—think of it as the opening to a vessel, and you are that vessel for divinity. When this chakra is unhealthy or closed, you feel disconnected from the Creator, alien, alone, and confused. The crystals that work with opening your crown chakra are selenite, clear quartz, and amethyst.

+ Please note that clear quartz works with and helps heal all chakras.

Journal Pause

- Which chakra(s) do you feel need the most healing at this time? Why?
- Which chakra(s) feel the most aligned or healthy at this time? Why?

We use our chakra or rainbow body to connect with the earth and the cosmos. All seven chakras combine to make the line you use to connect with crystals. The way we use chakras is best represented by two triangles intersecting, as in a Star of David.

The triangle that faces with the point down represents your three lower chakras: the root, sacral, and solar plexus chakras. These three lower chakras are connected to the earth's energy. They ground you. The root chakra (red) sits at the base of your spine, the coccyx area, and roots you directly to Mother Earth. This is where your instincts live. The sacral chakra (orange) is your womb or creation center. This womb is an emotional center. The solar plexus (yellow) is your inner sun. This is your place of power. These chakras all receive energy from Mother Earth and meet in your heart space. Your heart chakra (green) is your portal or bridge between the cosmos and the earth.

The other triangle of chakras faces upward. These upper chakras are your cosmic chakras, which connect you to divinity and your ability to channel. The first, at the top of your head, is your crown chakra (violet/white). This chakra is a thousand-petaled lotus that opens up God or Universe energy. This chakra allows you to ground, or root, into the cosmos just like the root chakra allows you to connect with Mother Earth. Next, the third eye chakra (indigo) is filled with this cosmic energy and opens for you to see clearly and beyond just the physical world. Then the cosmic energy travels into your throat chakra (turquoise), allowing what you perceive in your third eye to be expressed. Finally, the cosmic energy meets in your heart chakra (pink), mixing with the earthly energy. This combination creates a portal that opens you up and allows you to channel this energy from your heart center into your hands and use its magic.

The portal of your heart is an opening with all this spiraling energy. The heart chakra is where the earth and the cosmos meet within you, making you a living expression of "as above, so below." You have smaller chakras in the palms of your hands. They are both extensions of your heart chakra. Your left hand represents the divine feminine, or receiving, and your right hand represents the divine masculine, or doing. When you align your chakras, open your heart, and hold a crystal in your hand you are in perfect balance. This is the ideal state to be in to activate and connect with all crystals.

Clair-Senses

Before we discuss connecting with crystals, it's also helpful to know how you best connect with Spirit. We all have the ability to connect with the invisible or spiritual world, but there are different ways of doing so. You have probably heard the term *clairvoyant* used to describe a psychic. Clairvoyance is just one type of clair-sense. It's the ability to "see" beyond the 3D mundane. You have all the clair-senses but most likely have one that is more dominant than the others. You may feel that one of the senses is strongest, or you may feel inclined to a few. Here is a list of the most common clair-senses and how they manifest in the body while working with crystals.

+ *Clairaudience is clear hearing.* Clairaudience is the ability to really hear messages from your highest self, angels, and guides. It may be that you hear a voice in your head or that when you put yourself in the right state, you are able to allow your guides to speak through you. You may hear buzzing or ringing when you connect with a crystal, or you may hear messages.

+ *Clairvoyance is clear sight.* Clairvoyance is the gift of seeing messages. In the right state with their eyes closed, a clairvoyant can tune out the mundane world and tune into an inner world of pictures and symbols. Some see things almost like a movie or dream; others see stagnant pictures or only get glimpses. When you connect with a crystal, you may receive symbols, words, or images.

+ *Clairsentience is clear feeling.* People with clairsentience, when tuned in, feel the messages in their body. They may feel their heart race, or sense where someone was injured or where someone needs healing. Many people who identify as empaths sense the feelings of others in their own bodies. This kind of crystal connection may feel like butterflies in the stomach, a heart flutter, or a tingling in your hands.

+ *Claircognizance is clear intuition or knowing.* Claircognizance is the most common clair-sense. When you engage on a spiritual path, you find yourself just knowing certain truths. If you watch children, they often use this sense. They can't explain why they want something or don't want to go somewhere; they just feel it. With this type of a sense, holding a crystal may suddenly give you an answer, intuition, or clarity.

+ *Clairsalience is clear smell.* Someone who uses clairsalience registers phantom smells that are not present in the mundane world. They can smell incense or the perfume that someone who has passed on wore when they were on earth. When connecting with a crystal, you might associate the energy or healing with a smell. This smell can lead you to understand the crystal even more. For example, if you were to hold rose quartz and smell lavender, researching lavender would give you some insight as to what the rose quartz is offering you at that time.

+ *Clairgustance is clear taste.* Clairgustance is similar to clairsalience. The ability manifests as a taste, and these two abilities often manifest together. Taste is a tricky ability to connect with crystals, but the taste often leads you to a memory to trigger an understanding. You may notice you taste a sweetness for a loving feeling or bitterness for a crystal that might be helpful with shadow work.

+ *Clairtangency is clear touch.* Clairtangency is the ability to touch a person or object and receive information. Someone who uses this ability will hold an object and be able to reveal information about its history or owner. This type of sense is why most people prefer to hold the crystal they are working with. It gives a hands-on connection that can be harder to achieve without the crystal close to you and your heart chakra.

Journal Pause

- Which type of clair-sense do you feel is the strongest for you at this time? Which one fits the least? Why?
- What are some examples from your own past of clair or intuitive moments?

Knowing which of your clair-senses is most dominant can help you better understand which meditation practices work best for you. If you are clairvoyant, claircognizant, or clairaudient, guided visualization meditations tend to work really well. If you are dominant in your clairtangency or clairsentience, you feel deeply in your body and may require movement. You might need to engage in yoga or exercise or to not eat a few hours before your mediation practice. If you have a dominance in clairsalience, try lighting the same incense or diffusing the same type of essential oil before your meditation practice to help enhance and connect your ability.

Activating Crystals

I don't charge or program crystals. The idea of programming something feels manipulative and more like using than forming an alliance. Charging isn't something I feel is necessary once you know how to connect with and activate your crystals. Some crystals come to you completely awake, ready to heal, and lend you their energy. Others are sleepy due to mistreatment or being stored in darkness for too long.

RITUAL
Crystal Activation

You will definitely use this activation for any Spirit Crystals you obtain, but I also want you to know that this technique may extend beyond Spirit Crystals. You can use the following meditation for activating any and all crystals, stones, seashells, and even herbs. I am giving it to you now to practice before your Spirit Crystal enters your life. For now, just use any crystal or stone you already have with you for this exercise. Remember to only do this after your crystal has been cleansed. For a ritual like this, I would cleanse my space, open a ritual circle or sacred space, and call upon angels, guides, and deities to assist me. But not everyone reading this is a witch, so you can make this as ritualized or as minimalist as feels right for you. You might want to practice the Rainbow Breathing Meditation first as a way of connecting with your chakras and settling your energy.

When ready, first hold your crystal at heart level while standing or sitting. Close your eyes and take some deep breaths to center and calm yourself. Take as long as you need to feel ready.

Next, imagine your lower chakras connecting with Mother Earth. See yourself connecting with her and the energy flowing up in your heart center/chakra. Take your time. You can visualize or feel the energy of the earth however you would like. See it traveling up to your red root chakra at the base of your spine, then up to your orange sacral chakra in the womb area. Next the energy goes into your inner sun, your yellow solar plexus between your ribs and navel. Then the energy goes into your green heart chakra. It fills your chest and travels down your arms to your hands holding the crystal. Feel this earthly energy grounding you and rooting you down into the Great Mother.

Now see your upper self and chakras connecting with the Creator. This energy goes beyond the sky into the vast universe and beyond that. Visualize or sense this energy coming down into the crown of your heart. Your crown chakra opens like a many petaled lotus. Then this cosmic energy goes into your third eye, opening it to allow you to see clearly. Next, the energy travels into your turquoise throat chakra, allowing you to speak clearly. Finally, it travels to your heart center, meeting the earth's energy. Feel this energy swirling in your heart chakra and coursing into your hands.

Take a deep breath and say, think, or feel the following words:

Thank you, Mother Earth and the Creator, for meeting in my heart space. May your energy flow through me and into this crystal. May I be a vessel for this energy. May this crystal wake up to its purpose for the benefit of all, under the law of Grace. And so it is.

Visualize or feel the energy entering the crystal. The energy is both of the earth and the cosmos. It is not your energy; you are merely a vessel. Stay in this moment.

When you are ready, open your eyes, put the crystal down, and shake your body. Stamp your feet, shake out your arms, move your head yes and no, and release and ground the energy you have just been vibrating with. Take a moment to drink some water or have a snack to ground. Then journal about your experience.

Journal Pause

- Were you able to visualize or feel this energy? If so, what did it feel like?
- Did you feel, hear, see, or otherwise sense anything during this practice?
- Did you receive any messages from the crystal?
- How do you feel?

Some people have this amazing experience doing this activation, while others feel nothing. Neither is wrong. If you are concerned with whether you are doing it right, you are. If you really didn't feel like it went as well as it could, try again. Crystals are incredibly patient.

You may do this activation holding several of the same kind of crystal at once. In fact, in my classes, I often get asked if a person can activate more than one crystal at a time. The answer is absolutely. You can bring out your entire collection and activate them as a group. You might also want to try doing this activation in the sunshine for added energy.

Meditation Journeys

A journey is a type of meditation that is usually guided and allows you to journey as a soul. These are best practiced with an open mind. Each journey in this book requires you to set aside about twenty to thirty minutes of time you won't be disturbed. Read through the meditation journeys a few times, making modifications or changes as need be. If you want to record the following meditative journeys on your phone or other device, please do so. Decide on a comfortable place as well and whether you will be walking, sitting, or lying down. You want to also decide whether you would like to ritualize this journey with a candle, incense, or soft music, by opening sacred space and calling on deities, and so on.

It's also up to you whether you decide to do all of the following journeys back-to-back or spaced out over time. I suggest doing them in order over several days if possible. This way, if one of them doesn't go well, you can repeat it later that day or the next day before moving on to the next journey. But you may prefer to space them out over a longer period of time. Or you may want to wait and perform them on certain moon phases or power days. And yet you may only have one day off and feel confident in being able to do them all in one day. You decide, and as always, use your intuition.

These journeys will help establish the groundwork needed to later retrieve your Spirit Crystal. They are also creating a foundation for you to have a place in your mind where you can go to work with and communicate with your crystal. Each journey helps to expand your consciousness a bit more and open your intuition to receiving your Spirit Crystal. The biggest block people have to retrieving their Spirit Crystal is rushing the process. You are here because you want to truly bond with your Spirit Crystal and build a relationship. Like all good long-lasting relationships, you want to savor the process.

The Spirit Place

When going on a journey meditation, people will often establish a place in their mind's eye that they return to again and again. This is a Spirit Place. When I first began teaching this type of meditation, I would instruct people to go to a place in nature. But over the years, I have realized that this is limiting for some people. For some, their mind takes them to a galaxy. For others, they're transported to a cozy cabin. There is no wrong place to be. You might also find that your Spirit Place changes depending on what kind of journey you take. Be open to where your journey takes you.

MEDITATION
Discovering Your Spirit Place

In this meditation, I will guide you to a Spirit Place, and we will establish this place so you can visit over and over again. This place will be used in all of the journeys, so it's important to do it first and have a place established before moving on. This is also a great meditation journey to use whenever you need to rest or are feeling ungrounded.

Begin with a few deep breaths. When you feel relaxed, close your eyes or let your gaze relax. If thoughts arise, notice them and let them go.

We will start with a gentle body scan. I want you to focus on your feet, letting your feet relax and releasing any tension in your toes. Move your attention up to your legs, making sure they're comfortable, and release any tension, letting them rest. Now move your attention to your pelvis. A lot of us clench our pelvis during the day; let it melt and rest. Then let your belly and back relax. Next, allow each hand and all your fingers to release any tension and gripping. Moving your attention to your arms, let your arms go, rest, and just melt. Bringing your attention to your chest and upper back, release any tension. Release any tension you feel in your shoulders, neck, and jaw. Allow yourself to release your shoulders from your ears, maybe even opening your mouth a moment, sticking out your tongue, letting your jaw relax. Next, let your eyes relax. Let your whole head become heavy. Take a deep breath, and know that you are safe.

Now I want you to visualize yourself. This may be how you look in life or may be more of a soul version of you. I want you to see yourself, this other version of you that's going to go on this journey, this soul self, in your mind's eye, and we're going to take this version of you, your soul, self, or spirit itself, on a journey to a sacred space. You're going to begin by imagining your sacred self, your soul self, here with you. See yourself in the room or wherever you currently are.

Now, as I count down from five and get to one, you're going to see that self go through a big orb of light.

There is a big glowing orb of light, and your soul self, your higher self, is going to step through, leaving this place behind to go somewhere sacred, somewhere else, somewhere meditative. It's safe for you to do this. Let your body relax. You are in control. With a countdown to five, you will see this big glowing awe, and your soul self is going to go through this orb, this portal. Five. Four. Your soul self is getting closer to the portal, and it's glowing—glowing brighter and brighter. Three. Two. One. You are through the portal of light.

Where are you? Get a sense of this place. Look around. Feel, listen, smell. Get all of your senses involved. Wherever you are is your Spirit Place. Now, this may be a place you've actually been to. It could be a place on our actual earth. Or it may be a place on another planet, in another dimension, in another time and space. Take a moment as your soul self, your higher self, and look around. What colors do you see? What textures do you feel? What nature surrounds you? Are there trees? Are there animals? Is there water? Do you hear sounds? Is it day or night? You are safe. There's no wrong place to be. This is your place, your special place. It's your Spirit Place. And you can come here again and again to get guidance, to rest, to receive, to recharge. This place is unique to you. You are always safe here. Take another moment and look or feel around.

What do you see? How do you feel? Are there any messages coming for you here?

See your highest self sit down, smiling and comfortable. Your Spirit Place is so perfect for you. Let yourself sit for a moment in your Spirit Place and be recharged. Allow your breathing body to take deep breaths and your spirit self to be filled up. Know that you can return here anytime.

It is now time to return to your body in the here and now. Your spirit self walks from this resting place, and there's another portal. It is a big glowing orb of light, and your spirit self is going to walk through that portal. Leaving this place is just like arriving. On the countdown from five, you're going to be back in the mundane world. But don't rush. Your spirit self is approaching the orb. Five. Four. The portal is glowing brighter and brighter. Three. Your spirit self is walking through. Two. One. You are back in the here and now. Your spirit self is back in your body. You're back where you started. Take a moment to hear the sounds around you. Feel your body breathing. Take a deep breath. And when you're ready, open your eyes, stretch, and journal.

Journal Pause

- Were you able to establish a Spirit Place?
- What did it look like? What did it feel like?
- If you didn't discover or connect to a place, what changes can you make before you try again?

Spirit Guides

You might already have a Spirit Guide, animal guide, or guardian angel you work with. And if that is the case, I am happy for you! But I ask you to still try this journey. The guide you already work with may come through, but someone you've never met might too. The guide who is going to show you your Spirit Crystal may be someone totally new to you, and I ask that you go in with an open mind.

While this journey will help you meet the guide who will eventually help you retrieve your Spirit Crystal, I want you to put aside the desire to know your Spirit Crystal for now and try to focus solely on discovering and connecting with the guide. Later, when you are working with your Spirit Crystal, you may find that this guide shows up each and every time. The guide might serve as a sort of middleman or translator for your Spirit Crystal. Try to be open and patient.

MEDITATION
Discovering Your Spirit Guide

First, take some deep breaths, filling your belly with air, maybe putting your hands on your belly, and letting it out slowly. Close your eyes. Take as many deep belly breaths as you need. Remember that if thoughts arise or your body feels fidgety you can just remind yourself that you're human. Allow your body to melt. Relax your feet and hands so that they're no longer clenching or gripping. Feel your shoulders melt away from your ears. Open your jaw for a moment to release it. Close your eyes or relax your gaze. Be here now.

I'm going to provide a series of prayers, and I invite you to say them either aloud or in your mind. Feel free to modify them to fit your spiritual path:

> *Thank you to my Spirit Guide of highest consciousness.*
> *I thank you for being with me, and I look forward to connecting with you on this journey.*
> *I am open to receiving your guidance.*

You are now going to return to your Spirit Place. Visualize or feel your soul self standing in front of your body. Your body is relaxed, open, and ready to receive. Again, you are seeing that big glowing light, that big portal of energy that takes your soul self to your Spirit Place. Your spirit self is going to walk through there. With a countdown from five, you're going to go immediately to your Spirit Place. Five. Your spirit self is walking toward the portal. Four. You are almost in the portal. Three. You are crossing the portal. Two. One.

You are in your Spirit Place. Take a moment to watch or feel your spirit self, your highest self. Look around and re-establish connection. Be quiet for a moment and rest in your Spirit Place. Repeat the following prayer:

> *Divine source, the Creator, thank you for opening my third eye,*
> *my cosmic eye.*
> *Thank you for lifting any veil so that I may truly see.*
> *Thank you for clearing my ears so that I may truly hear.*
> *Thank you for opening my heart so I may truly feel.*

Imagine a flower at the top of your head, right at your crown. It could be a rose, lotus, or some other kind of flower. Visualize the flower petals opening as wide as they can. Then see light pouring into this flower at the crown of your head. Energy from the universe is going into your crown, into that flower, and into your body, allowing you to really open up. You are becoming a vessel, a channel so that you may connect and find your guide. Feel and sense that light going through your body. Take a breath.

No matter what kind of Spirit Place you have, visualize a cave or an opening like that of a cave. The cave is toward your left. You are on the outside of the cave. In a moment, your Spirit Guide is going to walk out of this cave. This will be the guide that leads you to your Spirit Crystal in the next meditation. Invite your Spirit Guide to emerge with the following prayer:

> *Thank you, my dearest Spirit Guide of highest consciousness.*
> *I am open to receiving your love, your light, your wisdom.*
> *I am open to your guidance and support.*
> *I invite you to join me now.*

Allow this guide to emerge. They may not be the normal guide you work with. They may not even look or be human. But this is the right guide for this time, in this meditation, in this journey. Take in your guide. What do they look like or feel like? What do you hear? What is the sense of this guide? Remember that you are safe. This is one of your guides. They are here for your evolution and healing. Repeat the following prayer:

> *Thank you, my Spirit Guide of highest consciousness, for revealing to me what I need to know at this time for my highest good and the good of all.*

Listen, feel, sense, or watch for a message. You may be seeing pictures or images, symbols, or words. Rest and receive your message. And if you don't receive a message, know that you might receive one later in a dream or through a symbol. You will now be returning. Thank your guide with words, a gesture, or an embrace.

Visualize your third eye gently closing, your ears closing, and the flower at the top of your head closing but not being closed off. It's just not being as open as it was for the meditation. Your heart is closing again but not closing off. Think of the closing as if each area is a door. You are leaving each door slightly ajar—not fully closed or open. Take a deep breath. See your spirit, self, and the portal of light. On the countdown from five, your spirit self is going to go back to the portal, back into your body, and back into the room. Five. Four. Your spirit self is getting closer to the portal. Three. Your spirit self is approaching the portal. Two. One. And now you're back. Take in the sounds around you. Take some deep breaths. Feel your body. And when you're ready, open your eyes. Journal what you heard, felt, or saw.

Journal Pause

Were you able to connect to a guide?

- If so, is it one you have connected to before?
- Can you describe your guide? (Write descriptions about or draw your guide.)
- Did you receive any messages?
- If you couldn't connect, why do you think that was?

In this chapter you became more aware of your chakras, found your Spirit Place, and were given instructions to meet a Spirit Guide. You also learned how to wake up or activate the crystals and stones you have in your life. I hope you are beginning to recognize your own energy as well as that of the crystals. You will connect with your Spirit Crystal on an energetic level. There will be an energy exchange that happens on your journey with your Spirit Crystal. Your Spirit Crystal will help you to see where you need to put your energy, what chakras need extra love, and what else needs healing at this time. I think it's time for you to retrieve your Spirit Crystal.

Chapter Three
Discovering Your Spirit Crystal

You picked up this book because you are ready to retrieve and connect with your Spirit Crystal. Skimming through the book, you may already have an intuitive impulse as to which crystal you connect with the most. You might have one of them in your collection already, but sometimes, people are surprised as to which Spirit Crystal comes through in the retrieval journey. It may not be one you feel drawn to, but it's the one that is drawn to you. It's important to be open to any of the Spirit Crystals as you move forward.

Our souls are infinite and ancient. Your soul has reincarnated many times on this planet as well as other planets. As you move through your incarnations and learn lessons, you create new soul contracts as well as soul missions. You chose this current life, parents, lessons, and the spiritual awakening. As your soul journeys, it has guidance. You have had the same guardian angel throughout all your lives. You may not believe in angels and may call them by another term, but they are with you nonetheless. You have others who travel and guide you as well: ascended masters, archangels, ancestors, galactic beings, animal guides, and a Spirit Crystal Guide. In this lifetime, you only have one Spirit Crystal. This doesn't mean you cannot connect with and work with the other crystals in this book. Instead, it means that one has been working to seek a connection with you.

Why Spirit Crystals

Prasiolite/aventurine, smoky quartz, rose quartz, clear quartz, citrine, and amethyst make up the family of Spirit Crystals. Spirit Crystals have come to us at this time because so many people are incarnating on the earth who have been here before. We are reincarnating now to help elevate and shift the energy of humanity for the better. The archetypes connected to the Spirit Crystals, which you were introduced to in chapter 1 and will learn more about in part 2, hold valuable lessons from the past of this planet and the people who once lived here. Remember that all rocks and stones are record keepers. But the strongest record keepers are all in the quartz family.

When you find your Spirit Crystal, you are given a key to understanding your soul's past and current purpose. Past lives are multidimensional, which means as you heal in this lifetime, you heal yourself in the past. This also means that you can learn from your past lives to help better yourself in your current life. Your Spirit Crystal will connect you with an archetype of the kind of person you can be. This is the person you can be when you heal yourself. In this chapter you will connect to your Spirit Crystal as well at its collective consciousness or soul.

Journal Pause

- At this time, which Spirit Crystal are you most drawn to?
- Which one are you least drawn to?
- Which archetype is most interesting to you? Why?

Meeting Your Spirit Crystal

Now is the moment you have been waiting for. But before you jump into the journey below, please make sure that you have established both your Spirit Place and Spirit Guide from the previous journeys. You will need both to establish a welcoming place for your Spirit Crystal to emerge.

MEDITATION
Retrieving Your Spirit Crystal

This is an exciting part of the book, and you may be feeling mixed emotions. You may be excited but also anxious, maybe a little fearful too. The best advice I can give is to go in with an attitude that you can always do it again if you feel it doesn't work out. This has been my attitude for all job interviews—I always treat it like it's practice, and this helps me relax and do well. The other piece of advice I want to offer is to be totally open to your Spirit Crystal. Don't go into this assuming you know which Spirit Crystal will come through. Just take on a beginner's mind and be as open as possible. Again, make sure you have established both a place and a guide before moving to this journey. In this journey, we rely on color. If you are color blind, then when I guide you to see color, ask to see or hear the word for the color or crystal instead.

I invite you to begin with three deep breaths. When you are ready, close your eyes and let your body be still for a moment. Instead of a body scan, you are going to tighten or clench up certain parts of the body in order to relax. You know your body best, so clench and tighten in ways that feel comfortable for you. Please do not hurt or strain yourself.

Begin with your feet. Flex your feet, whatever that means to you, whatever feels good for a moment, and then let them go and let them rest. Next, tighten the muscles in your legs. Clench them, and then let that tension go. Then clench your pelvis, your buttocks, and your abdomen, bringing them all in tight and letting them go. Make fists with your hands and curl your hands to your body, tightening and letting the tension go. Next, shrug your shoulders up to your ears and let that go. Then, tighten your face, making it look like you ate something sour, before letting that tension go and relaxing your face and jaw. Last, open your jaw like you are about to have a big yawn and stick your tongue out. When you are ready, close your eyes or soften your gaze.

Begin with a prayer:

Thank you, to Source, the Creator, for keeping me safe on this journey.
Thank you for helping me be creative on this journey.
Thank you for helping me stand in my power on this journey.
Thank you for helping me open my heart on this journey.
Thank you for helping me speak and hear the truth on this journey.
Thank you for opening my third eye—my cosmic eye—for this journey.
Thank you for opening my crown chakra, the flower at the top of my head, making me a vessel and a clear channel for this journey.
Thank you for opening my ears on this journey.

Visualize a rainbow of light coming down from Source, the Creator, to the crown of your head and down through each chakra. Then visualize your soul self. See them before you. You see and sense the portal that takes you to your sacred place. Your soul self is ready to step through. They approach the portal of light. On the countdown from five, your soul self will return to your sacred place. Five. Four. Three. Two. One. You are there. Look around and feel your secret space. To the left is the cave where your guide is waiting. You will invite them out with a prayer:

Thank you to my Spirit Guide of highest consciousness for joining me once again in my sacred place.
Thank you for guiding me to my Spirit Crystal. I am excited to know my crystal.

Your Spirit Guide emerges from the cave and greets you. They take you by the hand and lead you back to the cave from which they emerged. Here your Spirit Crystal will be revealed to you. You are at the entrance of the cave with your guide. You are safe. The entrance to the cave is dark, but you know that the entire inside of this cave is made up of your Spirit Crystal. In a moment, your guide will hold an orb of light, which you can use to reveal what your cave is made of. On the countdown from five, your Spirit Guide will hand you the light, and you will enter the cave to learn which Spirit Crystal is tracking you down, calling to you. Five. The orb of light is in your hands. Four. You are walking into the cave. Three. You are in the cave. Two. One. You are in the cave and holding the light. Look at the walls, the ceiling, and the floor of the cave. What do you see? Do you see a color, a texture, or a symbol? Do you hear or smell anything? What do you feel or sense?

Say the following prayer:

> *Thank you, Spirit Crystal, for revealing yourself to me.*
> *I am ready, I am open, and I am willing to receive you.*

If you're finding it hard to connect or concentrate or sense your Spirit Crystal, take some deep breaths and remind yourself to trust. Say, "I am open. I am willing to see." Touch the cave walls and ceiling, look for a loose crystal and hold it in your hand. What does it feel like? What is its weight, texture, temperature, and color? See if you can get an understanding of the color visually, as a sense, or by hearing the word. Take this Spirit Crystal piece and place it into your heart space—the middle of your chest, your sacred heart space, your chakra, the portal to all. Allow it to connect heart to heart with you.

Say the following prayer:

> *Thank you, Spirit Crystal, for coming to me.*
> *I am open.*
> *I am grateful and I trust.*

Take a moment to see if the Crystal has anything to reveal to you. Then when you are ready, thank the Spirit Crystal and leave the cave. Then thank your guide. Next, thank your Spirit Place, knowing that you can return here and connect anytime you would like. Notice the portal of energy waiting to bring you back. Approach the portal, and on the countdown from five, you will be back in the here and now. Five. Four. Three. Two. One. Take a deep breath and release any leftover energy. Let it dissipate into the earth below you. When you're ready, open your eyes and journal.

Journal Pause

– What color was your Spirit Crystal?

– Which emotion(s) do you associate with this crystal?

– If your crystal has a name, what is it?

– If it had a message for you, what was it?

Interpreting Your Retrieval

For some of you, the Spirit Crystal retrieval will be clear, but for others, the information received may be confusing. The following information is to help clarify murky visions or retrievals.

If you received a visual image of your crystal but no color and this is blocking your discovery, close your eyes and bring the images back and stay with them until a color comes. If this doesn't work, try the retrieval again or the automatic writing exercise below.

If you received color(s), read through the following list to match your color to the right crystal.

Color Interpretations:

+ *Clear, white, or rainbow:* clear quartz

+ *Red or pink:* rose quartz

+ *Orange, light brown, or yellow:* citrine

+ *Gray, dark brown, or black:* smoky quartz

+ *Purple, violet, or blue:* amethyst

+ *Green or greenish blue:* prasiolite/aventurine

If you received a name or word that doesn't match any of the names listed, try an internet search, as it may be a name for that crystal in another language. It may even be an anagram; try writing the letters down and rearranging them.

If you received a symbol for your crystal, know this is common for those who have had a recent incarnation on another planet (starseeds). Try looking up the symbol online or drawing it out and simply meditating on it. Gaze at the symbol with eyes relaxed and ask for clarification. You may also benefit from the alternative practice "Using the Crystals to Divine Your Spirit Crystal."

If you received what seems like more than one crystal—for example, the cave is green, but the crystal you take and put into your heart is purple—you could be confused as to which one is your Spirit Crystal. First, use your intuition and the journal questions to help you decipher. If you are still unsure, you can either do the retrieval again or use one of the other ways to discover your Spirit Crystal. But in this example, I would say the person's Spirit Crystal is amethyst, as it often grows in lava bombs that are green on the outside.

RITUAL
Automatic Writing to Discover Your Spirit Crystal

Automatic writing is channeling through writing. The meditation journey series is best for people who are able to get information through clairvoyance or clairaudience. For those who feel their information or have trouble with meditation for any number of reasons, automatic writing can be a great alternative.

For this practice, you will need a pen or pencil and some paper. You might also want to pick out six colored pens, markers, crayons, or pencils. Each color would represent one of the Spirit Crystals, and the color you are drawn to during the practice may be a clue as to which Spirit Crystal is calling to you. Using color is not necessary, though, so feel free to just use a pen if you prefer. It's best to use unlined paper since you may not stay in any lines if you have them. Which hand you decide to channel with is up to you. I use my normal writing hand, but you may have an intuition to hold the pen in your less dominant hand.

Next, make sure you can be in a quiet place, playing soft music if you wish, to limit distractions. Maybe light a candle or incense to set the mood, and open sacred space if that is in your practice. I would open sacred space and call in angels and guides, but this is your practice, so you decide how ritualized to make it.

Hold the writing utensil loosely. You can either close your eyes or keep them unfocused like you would to stare at a mandala. The key to any channeling is to relax. Take deep breaths, allow things to unfold, and don't give into anxieties or worries such as "Am I doing this right?" "Am I faking this?"

Start by writing the following question or a variation of it down on the top part of your paper: "Who is my Spirit Crystal?" Then relax and let your hand glide and move. You may feel a sense of what you're writing. You might hear a message in your head like a thought and write that down, or you may write without thinking first. You might even write without knowing what you are writing or drawing. There is no wrong way.

When you feel like the session is over, thank anyone you called in to help you, close your sacred space (if you chose to open it), and do something grounding, such as eating a snack or drinking some water. Then look over what you have written and try to determine what has come through. Sometimes, it's clear. Other times, it's a bit like a puzzle that takes a while to interpret. You can always refer to the "Interpreting Your Retrieval" section to help you.

RITUAL
Using the Crystals to Divine Your Spirit Crystal

I'm sharing this alternative for discovering your Spirit Crystal last for a few reasons. First, this option assumes privilege. You will need to obtain pieces of all six Spirit Crystals, and this may not be an option for everyone. The second reason is that not everyone is comfortable or familiar with the practice of divination, which is basically the art of fortune-telling. But for some of you, this may be the absolute best method to retrieve your Spirit Crystal, and in actuality, if you bought this book, you will probably buy all six crystals eventually anyway.

The first step is to buy all six types of Spirit Crystals. Next, you will need to cleanse and activate each one of the Spirit Crystals separately. You will need a dark cloth bag to put all the crystals into. Many rock shops sell velvet bags to store tumbled stones in, but you can use a bag meant for tarot cards or jewelry or make your own.

When you have everything ready, you will open sacred space, call on who it is you believe in and quiet yourself. You may want to take some deep breaths, meditate in your own way, walk around, or do something else until you feel you are in a calm and clear state.

Say something like, "My dearest Spirit Crystal, I am ready and willing to connect with you. Please reveal yourself to me at this time." Then close your eyes, reach into the bag, and pull out one crystal. Whichever one you choose is your Spirit Crystal.

Examine the crystal and use the journal pause after the retrieval meditation to answer questions about your crystal.

Spirit Crystals Choose You

The Spirit Crystals carry their own wisdom. There are no mistakes in connecting with a Spirit Crystal. Trust that you have been called to the right crystal or, more likely, the right crystal has called you. Spirit Crystals have deep wisdom. You have just begun your path with your Spirit Crystal! This is truly exciting. You are now empowered with the knowledge of which crystal has chosen you, and the journey begins to unfold now as to why you are connected. The why is where the true healing and wisdom come in.

Prasiolite/Aventurine

This beautiful green Spirit Crystal has chosen you because you are someone who is stepping into their wisdom. A sage is a wise person. Wisdom is where knowledge, experience, and intuition meet. Prasiolite in nature is rare, and it was the only crystal I questioned my guides about. That is when they presented me with aventurine. Aventurine can access the same consciousness as prasiolite and offers the same wisdom. Prasiolite/aventurine will guide you to step into your full power. Your power is in your wisdom. You are someone who others will seek out for advice. You hold good counsel and feel best when given lots of time and space to be alone. And if you just read this all and laughed because you feel there is no way that this description fits, then you have a bit of work to do.

Smoky Quartz

Smoky quartz varies in color. You may find a very light piece that is just a shade darker than clear quartz. Or you may find a piece so dark that it is hard so see through. Allow yourself to choose whichever you feel most drawn to. Smoky quartz chose you because you are brave. You are someone willing to face your fears in this lifetime in order to heal them. You are ready to let your shadows rise so that you may better understand yourself and evolve. A medium does not fear death. If you don't fear death, what is left to fear? If this description has made fear rise, then it is time to get to know your Spirit Crystal.

Rose Quartz

Rose quartz is such a beautiful crystal. It is a soft pink like a baby blanket. Sometimes it can be so pale it appears almost white. If you are like me, when you first read about the archetype lover, you may have heard the word sung in Taylor Swift style. A lover doesn't have to be a romantic lover. This archetype isn't about romance (unless you want it to be) but self-love and learning to love yourself so deeply and fully that you feel whole. It is about filling your cup so much that you have enough for others. You are an earth angel. Your love is healing. Trust the process, and your Spirit Crystal will help you open your heart.

Clear Quartz

Oh, to be a healed healer! Gone is the archetype of the broken healer who heals others while neglecting themselves. You have been through it in this life and others; there is no doubt. However, you will break the cycle. You will be a healed person in this lifetime. Clear quartz is so abundant on this earth that it often is overlooked. I recently received a crystal card deck that had over seventy cards and didn't include clear quartz. I was personally offended! Don't allow yourself to think that something being common makes it less valuable. Clear quartz is all over this earth for a reason. It keeps records and so do you. Working with clear quartz will open you to all of your possibilities.

Citrine

Citrine is such a hard-to-find crystal. What many people sell as citrine is often heat-treated amethyst. Real citrine is very light and clear. It is in between clear quartz and smoky quartz in color. This light gold crystal is your key to manifesting. A manifestor is not luckier than the other archetypes, nor are you greedy. A manifestor is a change maker. You are here to make changes for yourself and others. As you heal with citrine, abundance will follow. Not all abundance is monetary. You will learn to understand how to use your own inner power to help change your outer world.

Amethyst

Amethyst is a beautiful purple color and easy to identify and find. Amethyst calls you to become an alchemist. Alchemy is the energetic transmutation of something mundane into something magical. You're here to help change lower vibrations to higher ones. You are here to take wounds and turn them into lessons. You are here to transmute mistakes into wisdom. Like the priestesses and priests of ancient Egypt, you are here to once again step into your power and allow yourself to be gold.

I Know My Spirit Crystal—Now What?

It's time to get to know your crystal. I have a few fun suggestions for connecting further with your crystal in your own way. This connection helps open you up to your own intuition and also helps give you a deeper bond to your Spirit Crystal. The following exercises are a way of honoring this sacred bond.

Buying a Spirit Crystal

Earlier in this book you learned how to buy, cleanse, care for, and activate crystals. These same rules apply for your Spirit Crystal. The journey that follows will help you connect with your crystal. The type of crystal you buy is up to you. Tumbled crystals make for easier carrying and keeping with you. Raw crystals tend to be prettier. I would just avoid a carved crystal, such as a crystal skull, until you have already established a connection with your Spirit Crystal. There are many variations of the Spirit Crystals as well. For example, you might find that you prefer a chevron amethyst to a traditional amethyst. Go with your intuition as much as possible. Aventurine is much more common and easier to find than prasiolite. They are related, and this is why you can use them interchangeably.

MEDITATION
Connecting to the Collective
Consciousness of Your Spirit Crystal

Before you jump to the chapter on your Spirit Crystal, take a journey to connect to the collective consciousness of your crystal. For this journey, you will need a piece of your Spirit Crystal. If possible, either hold the crystal in your left hand or lay it in the center of your heart space. Close your eyes, take some deep breaths, and say, "Thank you to my Spirit Crystal (name the type) for allowing me to connect to you and all those crystals related to you. Thank you for allowing me to step into your grid."

Next begin to see, sense, or feel yourself back in your Spirit Place. Your Spirit Guide is waiting at the entrance of a cave. As you look at the cave, you realize that it is emitting a glow the color of your Spirit Crystal. Your Spirit Guide welcomes you and invites you into the cave. As you enter the cave, you see that the inside is made completely of your Spirit Crystal. In the center of the cave is a smooth crystal for you to sit upon. You sit on this crystal seat and immediately feel the aliveness of all the crystals around you. You can sense a frequency and vibration that is both healing and familiar.

The crystals begin to hum louder, and you are enveloped in their sound as well as their light. It's crystalline, prismatic, and the color of your Spirit Crystal. Allow yourself to be bathed in the frequency. This bath allows you to connect deeper to your Spirit Crystal and their grid upon the earth and beyond space and time. You suddenly see yourself in the middle of some sort of divine matrix or web. You are a point on this web, and all the other points are crystals. You are one with your Spirit Crystal. Now you may ask your Spirit Crystal for guidance and be open to what you receive. When you are done, return to your crystal seat in the cave. Leave your cave, thank your Spirit Guide, Cave, and Crystal. Then return to your body in the here and now.

Journal about your experience, and use this meditation as often as you like for a deeper bond with your Spirit Crystal and to receive guidance.

This Spirit Crystal cave is sacred to your own heart. Travel here to learn, grow, and receive messages. You may want to repeat this meditation daily, weekly, or on special power days to keep your connection with your Spirit Crystal strong. Your Spirit Crystal has much healing to give you but can only do so if you provide the space and time for the healing.

Connecting and Honoring Your Spirit Crystal Beyond Meditation

The following is a list of ideas of how to connect with your Spirit Crystal outside of meditation, divination, and rituals. Crystals like to be with us and a part of our lives. The best way to really connect with your Spirit Crystal is to keep it with you.

+ *Create a playlist:* This playlist can be based on how you see your Spirit Crystal, how it feels to you, what you think of when you see the archetype it's connected to, or the color. This can be a mix of spiritual music, including hertz frequencies, and popular songs. Just be open and let your intuition guide you. To help get you started, clear quartz makes me think of "She's a Rainbow" by the Rolling Stones. Smoky quartz feels to me like "Ouija Board, Ouija Board" by Morrissey. Amethyst feels like "Into the Mystic" by Van Morrison. Rose quartz definitely gives an "All You Need is Love" by the Beatles vibe. Prasiolite/aventurine feels like "My Sweet Lord" by George Harrison. "I Am Mine" by Pearl Jam fits citrine.

+ *Buy the crystal:* Use the first two chapters to help you find a good crystal. Cleanse and activate it. If you are truly having trouble finding your particular Spirit Crystal for purchase, you may use clear quartz as a stand in for any of them.

+ *Create artwork:* Use whatever medium you prefer—paint, fibers, charcoal, and so on—to create a piece of artwork that feels to you like your Spirit Crystal. It may be based off the color itself, the archetype, or something else.

+ *Build an altar:* I love a good altar (Taurus sun, Cancer rising here). An altar can be as grand as you can make it or as small as you need to fit or hide it. An altar gives you a place to rest your Spirit Crystal when you aren't working with it as well as a place to help remind you of this current practice. As you read the particular chapter on your Spirit Crystal, you will learn about more beings and allies such as herbs and other stones associated with it. For now, use your own intuition to add whatever you like. Some ideas are herbs, flowers, seashells, and other items found in nature; tarot cards; colored cloths; and symbols of your own beliefs.

+ *Take your Spirit Crystal on a walk:* Yep, you read that right. It's not a dog but it is an ally or friend. Take it out with you on a nice walk in nature. You can let it sit in the sun with you, give it a bath in a stream, or just simply keep it in your pocket.

+ *Keep it with you:* You can buy jewelry with your Spirit Crystal, sleep with it under your pillow, shower or bathe with it, keep it in your pocket, hold it while praying or meditating, and even talk to it. Just find a way to connect with it daily so you can strengthen your connection.

Journal Pause

– What is it you most want to know about your Spirit Crystal? Why?

– How will you connect with it and honor it?

– How do you plan on working with it daily?

– If you had to create a new word for your Spirit Crystal, what would it be?

– If you had to create a symbol for it, what would that be?

You now have your Spirit Crystal, a true friend and guide for life. I suggest jumping to the chapter on your Spirit Crystal, then going back and reading the rest of the chapters in chronological order. There are practices in each chapter that are beneficial for all of us—no matter our Spirit Crystal. As you read, you may find that you feel a powerful connection to a different Spirit Crystal or maybe even an aversion to one. This type of strong reaction should be honored. I personally work with all the Spirit Crystals and so can you.

PART TWO
The Spirit Crystals

Each of the following six chapters features a Spirit Crystal, but no matter which crystal chose you, you are encouraged to work with all of them. Each Spirit Crystal provides its own lessons for growth, evolution, and empowerment. Use these meditations, spells, and exercises to allow yourself to step into your most powerful, whole version of self. The prayer at the end of the introduction can be used to cast a protective circle before you embark on spellwork and ritual. If you already have your own process and prayer for casting a circle, you may still want to try this prayer, holding each of the crystals as you call in the directions. This process will help strengthen your relationship to the Spirit Crystals.

Each Spirit Crystal is connected to an archetype: the healer, alchemist, manifestor, medium, lover, or sage. You may see the label associated with your crystal and feel it just cannot be you. This is because the archetype is something that you evolve into. This process is much like how many people step more into the personality traits of their sun sign over their lifetime. You are evolving into your archetype through your spiritual journey and healing. Surrender to this possibility and allow your Spirit Crystal to guide you.

In the following six chapters, you will find special healing practices according to each Spirit Crystal. These chapters are focused on healing you from past-life wounds, reminding you of your inner magic, and guiding you to fully embody your archetype. There is power in the connection you have made with your crystal. Use this power to better yourself and your life.

Chapter Four
Prasiolite/Aventurine: The Sage

The term *sage* brings to mind a person like the figure in the traditional Hermit card of the tarot. A sage is a person who is wise, quiet, contemplative, and sought after for advice. Our Spirit Crystals choose us so that we may fully step into and envelope our archetype. You are a sage, even if you don't feel like one now. You once lived a deeply studious and meditative life in Shambhala. *Shambhala* means "place of peace" in Sanskrit. You are meant to know this inner peace now, here in this lifetime. Prasiolite or aventurine is here to guide you back to the peace that is your birthright. Moving forward, you can use prasiolite or aventurine or a combination of the two for the meditations, rituals, and spells. Prasiolite can be hard to find, and it's more important that you work with natural, undyed crystals. Prasiolite is also known as green quartz and can be so light in color that it looks almost clear. Aventurine is a richer green and much easier to find and works just as well.

When we think of the color green with a Western influence, we think of money. But green is the color of the heart chakra. Even though the chakra you are most connected with and have the most potential to open up is your throat, true wisdom travels from the heart to the throat. Knowledge comes from what you have learned from others, but wisdom comes from your intuition, experiences, and own insight. Wisdom comes from your heart. As you step into your sage self, this wisdom will develop. You will find answers to your own deeper questions, as well as answers for others if you choose to do so.

This chapter is dedicated to your healing and evolution as a sage. You will be given the tools that will help strengthen your relationship to prasiolite. As a soul on the path to remember being a sage and becoming one again, you will work on meditation to clear your mind and chanting to clear your throat chakra. You will open yourself up to abundance by revoking any vows of poverty that you took in a past life or this current one consciously or unconsciously. You will also begin or strengthen a path as a tea or herbal witch. Tea magic is a subtle magic but not one to underestimate on your healing journey. Tea rituals and magic will bring great healing to you and help you regain your inner wisdom.

Prayer for the Sage
Ancient and wise prasiolite, thank you for connecting to me.
I step into my wisdom.
I trust myself.
I listen to my inner knowing.
I feel my intuition.
I am wise.
I release any doubt.
And so it is.

Shambhala: Your Sacred Origin

Shambhala is a place of peace or silence. It's a sacred place outside of time and space, where the final incarnation of Vishnu awaits to incarnate for the golden age. Shambhala, like Lemuria and Atlantis, is viewed as a paradise. Souls that have had a lifetime in Shambhala are naturally clairvoyant, are fast thinkers, and understand true peace. Shambhala is in the past, the present, and the future simultaneously. This place transcends time as we understand it. So even though this was a place your soul lived in another lifetime, it doesn't mean that your soul will not return there.

Having lived a life in Shambhala can make the current world feel hard and confusing at times. You may get frustrated at how slow progress is toward peace in the world. You have a natural ability to "read" people and can often tell what they are thinking or feeling. You're empathic. You are quick to understand through listening and can pick up new languages easily. You find new technology and science fascinating, and you may be drawn to a field in tech or science. Careers where you can help others or the collective may also interest you. You prefer a quickness in your day, and this is why daily meditation is a key to help you achieve great balance.

Creating a Meditation Ritual that Works for You

Regardless of how you have felt about meditation in the past, your practice will get better and easier now that you know your Spirit Crystal. It's important for you to meditate daily with your crystal. This will build a strong bond and also help open you up to your own inner wisdom. Sitting in meditation is a receptive gesture to the Creator. You are in essence like an empty bowl or cup. You are allowing yourself to rest in order to be filled with light, energy, and magic. It doesn't matter if you decide to meditate for five minutes or one hour every day. It doesn't matter if you decide to do walking, sitting, guided, nidra, breath, or any other kind of meditation. What matters is that you commit to a practice and that you have your crystal with you each and every time. This practice is key to your own healing and soul evolution.

To help make this practice become a habit, pick a moment of the day that you know you have the time for meditation and stick to it. If you have to, write it in your schedule or set a reminder on your phone. Practicing at the same time will create routine, and eventually your ego will stop fighting against what your body is doing day after day. Using the same incense or essential oil scent each time you meditate will also help strengthen the habit because scent is so deeply connected to memory. Depending on what kind of meditation you choose, you might want to pick the same music to listen to each time. This will also help set the tone for your body and mind, letting you know you are transitioning into meditation. Last, if you are fortunate enough to have a space you can set up to meditate in every day, this will further strengthen the routine. It doesn't have to be fancy; it could be a cushion you store under your bed and pull out every day to use or even your yoga mat after you exercise your body.

Journal Pause

- What is your current relationship to meditation?
- What do you think is valuable in a meditation practice?
- What has prevented you from creating a meditation practice?

Green Tara

One of the aspects for the Creator that is connected with prasiolite is Green Tara. Green Tara is one of the Taras or stars of Buddhism. Green Tara is the most protective and compassionate of the Taras. She was born from a river of tears in which a lotus grew. From this lotus, Tara sprung to life. The lotus is revered because it is a beautiful flower that grows in the mud. The lotus symbolizes growth and enlightenment from suffering. Green Tara is a bodhisattva, which means that she has chosen to help humanity evolve and become enlightened. She is the great liberator and is here to help free us from suffering and the wheel of reincarnation, or samsara. She is also a goddess of mystics; *mystic* is another term for sage.

If you decide to work with Green Tara, you can find a variety of statues, prayer flags, and incense created in her honor. These things are not necessary but might enrich your path. To connect with Green Tara, use her sacred chant. It is *Om Tare Tu Tare Ture Soha* (pronounced ohm tarey too tarey turey swvaah ha). This chant means "I prostrate to Tara the liberator, mother of all the victorious ones." You are being liberated by chanting this mantra. You are asking Tara to free you and open you up. Here is a prayer you can also use to connect with her:

> *Om Tare Tu Tare Ture Soha.*
> *Green Tara, enrobe me in your light of emerald.*
> *Fill each one of my chakras with your light,*
> *Breaking them free of cords, ties, and bindings.*
> *Thank you for freeing me of what no longer serves.*
> *Thank you for helping to clearing my throat chakra.*
> *Guide me to speak the truth.*
> *Guide me to speak freely.*
> *Om Tare Tu Tare Ture Soha.*

Kuan Yin

Kuan Yin, or She Who Hears the Weeping, is a bodhisattva of love and compassion. Her story is one of transformation on many levels. Her name has different variations throughout Asia, and her gender has changed overtime as well. She is a transgender being of light. She was severely mistreated by her father but always chose forgiveness and compassion, elevating her to a bodhisattva in death, much like the elevation of good souls to sainthood in Western culture.

Kuan Yin's energy is so soft and loving that connecting with her feels like a good hug. If you decide to work with her, you can find beautiful necklaces, statues, and other artwork created in her honor. You can also connect with her by sitting in meditation and asking her to take you to her island, P'u-t'o Shan. Her island is a sanctuary of peace and love. Sit in meditation, say her mantra, and envision yourself meeting Kuan Yin in her sacred place. Kuan Yin's chant is *Om Mani Padme Hum* (pronounced ohm manee pad-may hoom). This mantra translates to "the jewel is in the lotus." This mantra is considered one of the most powerful chants ever to be spoken. Your crown chakra is the thousand-petaled lotus, and when healthy and open, it allows you to connect easily to the Creator. The jewel is your soul. You can also use the following prayer to connect with her:

Om Mani Padme Hum.
Beautiful and wise Kuan Yin,
Compassionate bodhisattva.
Thank you for opening my heart wide.
May compassion enter my heart space and spread through my being.
May I be compassionate with myself, friends, relations, lovers,
    strangers, and enemies.
May compassion lead to forgiveness and forgiveness lead to wholeness.
With your guidance, I forgive myself.
I forgive those who have wronged or hurt me.
In forgiveness, I am free.
Om Mani Padme Hum.

Your Crystal Allies

Prasiolite is your Spirit Crystal, but it has companions. The following are crystals that work best with your Spirit Crystal and will enrich your healing journey.

Sodalite is a sweet little stone that is quite common and looks like a well-worn pair of blue jeans. Sodalite's healing lies in the connection it can give you to your intuition. A true sage combines wisdom and knowledge, intuition and logic. Sodalite's gentle energy helps unite the head with the heart. Keep it with you while meditating, journaling, and dreaming. Its energy is subtle, so you can work with it daily. It is also great for gridding—more on that in the last chapter.

Jade comes in many colors, not just the green that is commonly worn by many. You have probably seen circular pieces of green jade worn on necklaces for protection and wealth. A necklace like this would make a wonderful talisman for a sage. The circle symbolizes infinity, representing the constant rebirth cycle. Wear it near your heart with the intention to step into your soul self. Jade, aventurine, and prasiolite all blend their energies well. Allow your jade necklace to rest with your Spirit Crystal to gain more energy.

Blue tiger's eye is less common than the orangey brown we see so often but still relatively inexpensive. If you can, buy many little tumbled pieces and use them in grids on your altar. You may also want to hold them in your hands while meditating because they help produce a deep calm. You will find their energy subtle, and they work quite well with sodalite.

Amber isn't actually a crystal. It's fossilized tree resin or sap. However, it is powerful for a sage. Worn on the skin, amber starts to release some of its resin. It has a delicious and subtle smell. Amber is wise and calm like a true sage. Trees are the planet's sages. Wear amber beads in honor of the wisdom of the trees and to promote a natural calm.

The Throat Chakra

Your throat chakra is your healing and power center. A healed sage has an open and almost golden throat chakra. The healing practices here, which include chanting and drinking tea, will help open, remove blocks from, and heal your throat chakra. Chanting will help you speak your wisdom more freely. Tea has subtle plant medicine that helps to coat the actual throat and change the vibration of this part of your body both physically and in the chakra. If you find yourself unable to speak your truth at times, gently rest your left hand on your throat and take a deep breath. This subtle touch will remind you to speak from this chakra.

MEDITATION
Chanting with Green Tara and Kuan Yin

Your throat chakra, when healthy, allows you to voice your truth and wisdom with confidence and clarity. But oftentimes the throat chakra can become sluggish when we aren't in the practice of sharing our wisdom. Chanting a mantra clears and opens the throat chakra through the repetitive vibration. For this meditation, you will need a set of prayer beads with the traditional 108 beads or a rosary. If you can, find a mala made from aventurine beads or one of the companion crystals listed earlier. You can also string your own prayer beads for added intention. First, if you haven't done so, cleanse your mala or rosary with sacred smoke; you can do so by burning a dried bay leaf. Run the beads across the smoke three times. If your prayer beads are not made from crystal, then gently wrap them around a piece of prasiolite or aventurine and call on your Spirit Crystal to imbue your beads with its energy. Otherwise, hold the crystal beads in your left hand and ask them to wake up and activate just like you have done with crystals previously.

Once your beads are ready to use, choose a chant that feels right for you at this time. You can choose Green Tara's mantra, Om Tare Tu Tare Ture Soha, or Kuan Yin's chant of Om Mani Padme Hum. Or you might have one you feel more drawn to at this time. After you have chosen a mantra, sit or stand in a comfortable manner and hold your prayer beads. Close your eyes and take a deep breath, then begin chanting. As you touch each bead, say the mantra. Do this with each bead until you have completed the entire mala or rosary. You can practice chanting in different ways. You might enjoy a pattern of chanting in your head, whispering, and speaking. You might enjoy singing the chant and can find many free tracks on streaming services with chants to sing along to. As you develop your practice of chanting, you will begin to feel clarity after your sessions. You will begin to tune into the vibration of your own voice within your body. You will also notice that it is hard to have a busy mind while chanting, so this practice is great for when you are anxious or stressed. You can also use your chanting to clear your space and objects much like you would use sacred smoke or Reiki.

Sacred Number One

Your sacred number as a sage is one. One is not the loneliest number. One represents the self, individuality, independence, leadership, and being at one with yourself and all that is. The number one invites you to welcome the different parts of your mind to come together and create one consensus. One is the beginner's mindset and the ability to begin again whenever you need to. One symbolizes your need for quiet meditation and time to go within. The Magician is the one card of the tarot. In the card illustrated by Pamela Colman Smith, he is shown as the master of the four elements, standing strong and powerful. You are this master. You are magic.

RITUAL
Healing Lack

A common issue for those who have had past lives as monks or nuns is that they have taken a vow of poverty. You may have had a past life as a monk or nun or perhaps had another reason to take a vow of poverty. This vow often stays with a soul from lifetime to lifetime. This vow might translate as poverty in a number of ways, not just financially. In this ritual, you will renounce any vows of poverty and release yourself to be able to attract abundance in this lifetime. This ritual is best done on or around a new moon. You will need matches or a lighter, a green or white candle in a small jar or tea light form, allspice (from a grocery store is fine) for luck and money, basil (dried) for money, cinnamon for prosperity and protection, and a bay leaf to purify. You will also need a small piece of prasiolite or aventurine as well as a piece that is shaped into a point (if you don't have one like this, then a toothpick can work).

Before the ritual, set up an altar with a space for your candle to burn down safely until it goes out on its own. Next, prepare your candle. First, cleanse your candle by burning the bay leaf, allowing the smoke to envelope the candle. Next, use a pointed crystal or toothpick to write your full name on the candle. Then either press in or sprinkle on the herbs listed. When it comes to herbs, a little goes a long way on candles. You don't want to set your candle on fire with the dried herbs but want to enhance the magic of the candle with them. Press the small piece of prasiolite or aventurine into the candle away from the wick (once the candle burns down, you will be able to retrieve the crystal and clear off the wax to use it again).

When all is set up, open sacred space and take a deep breath. Say, "I call on my highest self, my soul self, to step forward. I call on my angels and Spirit Guides of highest consciousness to join me and bear witness. I call upon my ancestors. I call upon my Spirit Crystal to guide and assist me. I thank the herbs and crystals present with me. I am here to release myself from any vows of poverty." Take a deep breath and close your eyes. Allow yourself to feel the vow of poverty and lack rise to the surface. You may see it as an empty bag or cup. You may see the life in which you took the vow, or you may just feel it. Then open your eyes and say, "I release the vow of poverty I once took. I renounce any vow, soul contract, or ancestral curse related to poverty. I do not need to be poor in this lifetime to be spiritual. This vow is no longer serving my highest good, and I invite the mighty Green Tara to come in and cut me free. Thank you, Green Tara, for cutting this vow from my soul and releasing me." Now light your candle and take a moment to gaze into the flame. Feel the flame burning away this vow of poverty with the help of Green Tara. Now say, "I am free. I am free to be abundant. I am free to know wealth in this lifetime. I am free to be full. Thank you, Green Tara. Om Tare Tu Tare Ture Soha."

Thank those you called upon, close your sacred space, allow your candle to burn down, and then take some time to journal.

Journal Pause

- What does it mean to be abundant?
- What does it mean to be rich?
- Where in your life do you have abundance?

Your Plant Allies

Teas of all kinds are sacred and helpful for your overall well-being and spiritual journey as a sage. Try green, white, and black teas until you find the one that you enjoy best. They have different caffeine levels, and you can also find many caffeine free. White tea is extremely helpful if you suffer brain fog or other lower energy disorders; it is a low caffeine tea you can drink throughout the day. In the following paragraphs, we will look deeper at a few specific plant allies for your archetype healing.

Bay is easily found and a wonderful cleanser. You can find the leaves at grocery stores and burn them to cleanse your space or items. Keep a leaf in your wallet to increase and keep your abundance. Add it to food and teas for protection.

Sage is an overall cleanser. Avoid buying white sage, as it is overharvested and used in certain closed practices sacred to Indigenous peoples of North America. Instead, you can use the regular grocery store variety for cleansing yourself and your space.

Basil is not only delicious in pesto but useful for money and abundance spells. Make a tincture and wipe down your front door to bring money into your life on a new moon. Tend to a plant on your altar when working on money spells.

Spearmint is an overall healer. It settles tummies, brings good dreams, improves headaches, and helps add focus to spellwork.

Lemon balm is easy to grow, great in teas, and an overall immune booster. Your immune system may need help from time to time and lemon balm is a tasty boost of health. Lemon balm is a natural antiviral and helps soothe and balance the mind.

Lotus flower tea helps reduce stress and lower blood pressure. Drink it to remind yourself that great beauty and wisdom rises out of the mud.

RITUAL
Daily Teatime

A daily tea ritual will help you remember your purpose and who you are evolving into again in this lifetime: a sage. Tea is a potion. Drinking tea can be both a meditative and a magical experience. For this ritual, you will need your Spirit Crystal, your favorite tea, and an herbal ally that you would like to work with. Adding sage to your tea will bring a sense of peace and calm—perfect before a meditation. A bit of basil in your tea will bring abundance and luck. For increased psychic powers, try a bay leaf. For overall health and protection, try some lemon balm. You have a natural inclination to understand and work with herbs. Tap into this intuition and begin to experiment with tea blends and infusions. Once you have your tea and herbs chosen, set up an area in your kitchen to work. You will need your prasiolite, intention, a teacup, your chosen tea, chosen herbs, a spoon, a lighter or match, and a candle (green is best but you choose). You can even set up a small altar in your kitchen and use a tall seven-day candle that you can light and reuse day after day.

Next, open sacred space and mindfully, with full presence, put your water to boil, light your candle, and place your crystal in your teacup. Take a deep breath and say, "Thank the elements of water and fire for coming together to create my tea. Thank you, element of earth, for nourishing these plants in your soil. Thank you to the air within my lungs for giving me the breath of life." Now take a deep breath and hold your intention for your tea in your mind and gently exhale into your cup and onto your Spirit Crystal. Then say, "Thank you to my Spirit Crystal for lending your wisdom and magic, infusing my tea with the (fill in what is the purpose of your tea blend; it could be, for example, health). Earth, air, fire, and water happily meet within me and around me. May it be so." Remove your crystal and set it next to your cup. Add your tea, herbs, and water and allow the tea to steep. When the tea is ready to drink, drink slowly and mindfully. Keep your intention in mind. When you have finished your tea, thank the elements and your Spirit Crystal and close sacred space. Don't throw your tea remnants down the drain. Instead, compost them, put them in the garden, or release them in some other natural way. You don't want your magic going down the drain or in the trash.

Journal Pause

- What is your favorite tea at the moment?
- What are some tea blends you would like to try?
- Could you create a little kitchen or tea altar? If so, how?

Reading Tea Leaves

Tea leaf reading is a natural form of divination for a sage. After performing your daily tea ritual, leave your loose tea at the bottom of your cup. If you used a tea strainer, pour some of the wet leaves into your cup. Then turn your cup upside down onto a saucer. Take a deep breath, close your eyes, and rotate the cup clockwise until you feel satisfied. Open your eyes, turn your cup right side up, and gaze. Tea leaf reading takes patience and practice. Look for shapes, symbols, letters, and numbers. It helps to let your eyes relax in drishti. Then record what you see with words or draw the shapes you see. Resist the urge to look up any symbols' meanings, and instead let this be a practice of honing your intuition. For example, if you saw a bird, allow yourself to think about all that a bird could symbolize. Keep from looking up what other people say a bird symbolizes. This pull to look up information is natural in our society, but it won't help you tap into your own wisdom. Then as the day unfolds, reflect back on what you saw in your cup and see if you can now attach a meaning.

Trust the Sage Within

No matter where you think you are on this journey to becoming a sage, I am sure it is further than you believe. Continue to repeat the practices in this chapter until they become ingrained rituals in your daily life, then continue to explore. Allow your intuition and the communication you have with prasiolite to guide you. Be open to insights and new studies. Lifelong learning suits you and will bring you comfort and joy. To be a true sage is to give into your inner guidance. Allow yourself to be wise.

Notes on Prasiolite/Aventurine

The following is a list that will help you go further on your path to becoming a sage. Use this list as a way to explore your archetype and create magic and rituals of your own.

+ *Important past life:* Shambhala
+ *Deities associated with this crystal:* serpents, dragons, reptiles, buddhas, and bodhisattvas, especially Kuan Yin and Green Tara

+ *Plant allies:* bay, sage, basil, spearmint, green tea, lemon balm, other tea blends, and lotus flowers
+ *Crystal and stone allies:* sodalite, jade, blue tiger's eye, and amber
+ *Divination tool:* tea leaves
+ *Sacred number:* one
+ *Direction:* south
+ *Element:* fire
+ *Chakra:* throat

Chapter Five
Smoky Quartz: The Medium

S moky quartz chooses to guide those who can become mediums in this life-time. A traditional medium is someone who can make contact and receive messages from those who have crossed over or passed away. Being a traditional medium isn't always safe. Many mediums will feel drained after reading for others, and some even suffer temporary blindness. This is because some mediums allow the ghosts and spirits to attach to them to share a message. We will focus on how to be a healed and protected medium, one who can heal without becoming cursed. But more importantly, smoky quartz has come to teach you how to truly live your life to the fullest while understanding, embracing, and no longer fearing death.

Stepping into your potential as a medium means facing your fears. All fears can be broken down into two categories: a fear of living or a fear of death. If you are afraid or anxious of making a mistake, that is a fear of living, whereas if you are afraid of falling from a great height, that is a fear of death. A healed medium doesn't fear death. They know that death is just a portal to the next stage, and after death, there is peace. This doesn't mean that you are to be fearless but instead that you will walk side by side with your fears. You will be aware of them, but you won't let them limit you. You will push past them and live a brave life.

Being a healed medium doesn't have to lead to speaking to dead people. It will instead lead to freedom. When you continue to face and release fears, you free yourself. In this chapter, you will receive the healing tools you need to evolve on your path. You will connect with Jaguar, Archangel Azrael, and Hekate to help you release what is no longer serving you. You will learn how to remove unwanted guests who have attached to your chakras to drain your energy, and you will learn how to move your body to remove stuck energy. You will also find a ritual to help you release the fears that block you from living your life. You will have the essential tools you need to begin healing.

Prayer For the Medium
I bravely connect to the rainbow bridge.
Smoky quartz is within and around my being.
I walk hand in hand with death.
Free of my fears, worries, and doubts.
I am a bridge.
I am a conduit.
I am safe here and now.
And so it is.

Understanding Paititi

Smoky quartz is connected to Jaguar and saints, angels, and gods and goddesses of death. It's also associated with the ancient Incas. The Incan shamans could reach a land called Paititi (PIE-tee-tee), or the city of gold. This is a Spirit Realm that one can access for healing and wisdom. This spiritual place was misunderstood by the conquistadors to be a literal place of gold, which they called El Dorado. The gold is already within you. You have the ability to track down and release fears in this lifetime. You are connected to Paititi. Your soul has recognized this great place as one you need and can access for your own healing.

Jaguar and the West

As a medium, Jaguar is a power animal that can help you evolve. Jaguar is an apex predator of North and South America. She can be golden with dark rosettes or melanistic with subtle spots. In shamanism of the Andes, Jaguar is the mother and sister who resides in the South. She is the one who comes to help us face our fears and our companion who helps us cross the rainbow bridge when our bodies die. She has nothing to fear. She is a being who will help you face and release your fears. To connect with her, set up an altar facing the west. On this altar, place a piece of artwork that depicts a jaguar. It's best if you create it yourself. She doesn't care if you don't consider yourself an artist. Another way to connect with her is to take her for a walk. Allow yourself to embody and become a jaguar. Put on music and move the way she would move. This dancing of the animal goes back a long time and may seem silly in modern times but is actually extremely powerful. Use the following prayer to connect with Jaguar:

Mother, Sister, Jaguar of the west,
The guardian of the rainbow bridge,
Fearless predator of the dark jungle.
Thank you, Jaguar, for being at my side.
Thank you for guiding me to track down my fears and face them.
Jaguar, protect me on my journey into the underworld of my own self.
Jaguar, lend me your medicine of courage.
Mother, Sister, Jaguar, make me brave so that I may lead a life of love,
Free from the shadows of fear.
Aho!

I do want to make a note that the term *power animal*, like *spirit animal*, is not to be used flippantly. The term here is used with reverence and in honor of Jaguar, who is one of the four power animals of shamanism in South America. If you don't feel a connection to Jaguar in this lifetime, you may want to connect with a big cat that lives near your land. In North America, that might be a mountain lion.

MEDITATION
Connecting to the Rainbow Bridge and Entering Paititi

Calling on Jaguar in this meditation allows you to have a companion to keep you safe while you travel and enter Paititi. Paititi is another realm, another world within our world. You can enter this golden place to learn, heal, and find freedom, but you need a guide. Before this meditation, open sacred space and have a smoky quartz in your left hand or placed upon your heart center.

Close your eyes and take deep breaths. Allow your body and mind to relax. Envision and feel yourself being surrounded by the frequency and light of your smoky quartz. Know that your Spirit Crystal is placing you in a protective orb but also raising your frequency so that you can travel easier in your mind and spirit. Allow yourself to travel back to your Spirit Place. Take a moment to see, feel, and sense your Spirit Place. Know your body and mind are safe.

Now, invite Jaguar to join you in your Spirit Place; call on her with respect and kindness. "Jaguar, mighty protector, guide, and healer, please join me in my sacred place. Join me on my quest to find the city of gold. Thank you for your protection and patience." Everyone's Jaguar guide appears differently to them. See and get a sense of your guide. What color(s) is your Jaguar. Notice their eyes. What gender are they? Is she giving you a name? Take a moment to know this mighty guide.

Now follow your Jaguar. They are leading you softly and swiftly from your Spirit Place, but you know you are safe with them. You follow Jaguar on a path that goes through different terrain and seasons. The path continues on to what seems like the end of the world that you know. You are coming to a place where the path ends and a rainbow bridge begins. The rainbow is translucent and filled with light. It is vast and beautiful. You wait at the edge with Jaguar, and they let you know that this bridge will take you to the place you seek: Paititi. Jaguar will not follow you, as they have served their role as guide, but know that your Spirit Crystal is with you.

You step onto the bridge believing you will walk, but you soon realize it is more like a river. You begin to swim. As you swim, all the things you cannot bring with you to Paititi are rinsed away. You come to the end of the rainbow and are in the land of gold. You look down and realize you are in your light or luminous form. Your body has been left in the rainbow water to be reclaimed upon your return.

You take a step into Paititi and begin to allow yourself to observe. What do you see? What do you sense? How do you feel? You are safe here, in a place beyond space and time. As you look around, you realize a golden box sits before you. You know this box is meant for you. You kneel and pick it up in both hands. It is light even though it is solid. You know that when you open the box a gift will be revealed to you in the form of a symbol that you will understand. This gift is your gift. This is your gold. It is the gift within your heart. Take a deep breath and open the box. What do you see? What do you feel? What do you hear?

Gently scoop up what is inside of the box and place it into your heart center. Give thanks to Paititi for revealing your gold. Then close the box and set it back on the ground. It is time for you to return now. Walk back to the rainbow bridge and enter your body. Allow the current to take you back to Jaguar, who has patiently waited for your return. Step out of the rainbow and walk with Jaguar up the path you came from, back to your Spirit Place. Thank Jaguar for their guidance, and thank your Spirit Place. Thank your Spirit Crystal and begin to take deep breaths. Feel your body, notice the sounds and temperature of the room you are in, and open your eyes. Journal about your experience, close your sacred space, and drink water or eat a snack to ground yourself.

Journal Pause

- Write down what you can remember from this meditation.
- What did your Jaguar look like?
- What did you notice in Paititi?
- What was your gift? Why do you think this gift came to you?

The Angel of Death

Another being that can help you in your evolution as a medium is Archangel Azrael. Archangel Azrael is the angel that helps souls cross over to the other side at their time of death. Azrael is a beautiful angel with raven-like wings and a comforting, soft energy. He is always willing to assist us with any kind of change or transformation we are going through. There is no need to fear Azrael, as he is our friend in life and death. I associate him with crows and ravens, and whenever I see them, I know he is with me. To honor him, simply begin calling on him and talking to him. Angels are very easy to connect with and don't need particular altars or offerings. Use the following prayer to connect with him:

Thank you, Archangel Azrael, for placing me in your dark ruby-red light of protection.

Thank you, Azrael, our friend in death, for being with me now.

Guide me, Azrael, to face my own death in life.

Thank you for guiding me to let the parts of me die that are no longer serving me.

May I be free to live in this lifetime.

With you by my side, I am free to truly live.

I invite my soul self forward.

I walk the path of my soul unafraid of what awaits me.

Amen.

Journal Pause

- How do you feel about angels?
- What—if anything—is holding you back from working with them?

RITUAL
Releasing Hitchhikers

As a soul that connects easily to the rainbow bridge and beyond, you easily pick up unwanted spirits and guides. Everyone has a team of Spirit Guides. This team consists of animals, a Spirit Crystal, angels, ancestors, ascended masters, deities, soul family, and elementals. Bigger teams are often attached to older souls but not always. Many people wish to connect to their guides, but what not everyone realizes is that not every member of their team is positive, helpful, or of the highest consciousness. Think about the old proverb "too many cooks spoil the broth." This can be the case with your Spirit Guides. Not everyone traveling with your soul is helpful. These unhelpful guests are essentially hitchhikers attracted to your soul, chakras, and vibration.

As you evolve on your spiritual journey, it's essential to go through your team of guides and remove those who are not serving your highest good. In this ritual, you will use your smoky quartz to cut away and draw out the hitchhikers and then call upon Archangel Azrael to help you release the entities who are not serving your highest good. He is here to help those souls attached to you to find their way to the afterlife.

For this ritual, you are going to need a pointed or terminated piece of smoky quartz. You will also need a black or purple candle, a lighter or matches, and a cleansing herb or incense to burn, such as copal, bay leaf, mugwort, or sage (do not use white sage; it is endangered and for closed practices only). This ritual is best performed on a new moon. When you are ready, use your sacred smoke to cleanse yourself, the space, your crystal, and your candle. Cast a ritual circle or open sacred space. Light your candle and sit with your terminated smoky quartz in your hands.

Say, "Thank you to my Spirit Crystal for being with me. Thank you for enveloping me in your smoky light. I am protected and cleansed in your essence." Visualize yourself in the frequency and light of your smoky quartz. Then say, "Thank you, Archangel Azrael, for joining me in this ritual. I take comfort in your presence. I ask that you stay with me and guide this ritual." Visualize or sense Azrael joining you. I often see his energy as a deep red.

Face the point of your crystal toward your heart space and say, "I thank my Spirit Crystal and Archangel Azrael for removing any entities, hitchhikers, guides, or other beings attached to my soul, spirit, and chakras who are draining me, holding me back from evolution, or are no longer serving my highest good." Then feel and sense the crystal drawing out sluggish, dark, or uncomfortable energy. "Thank you, Azrael, for assisting these beings in their leave. I thank you, Archangel Azrael, for removing and releasing anyone who is not for my highest good from my team of guides." Allow Azrael to surround you in his red light and know that you are safe. When you feel the process is complete, say, "Thank you to my Spirit Crystal and Archangel Azrael, and thank you to my Spirit Guides of highest consciousness for guiding, guarding, and protecting me. And so it is."

Next, take your crystal and run it over the flame of the candle (be careful) and envision whatever you drew out of your heart center dissolving in the flames. Close your circle and journal about your experience. Place the crystal either in a pot of dirt or outside in the sun to cleanse even further.

Hekate: Goddess of the Crossroads

Hekate was a Titan in mythology and has been reclaimed by many as a goddess. Hekate is fierce and ancient. Hekate is a wonderful protector, especially of those who identify as non-binary or female. Hekate is the goddess of witchcraft, crossroads, the night, and magic. She is strong, dark, and mighty. For you, the medium, Hekate can help protect and guide you on this path. You can work with her to help unlock your true potential, as she is also the keeper of the keys. To honor her on your altar, place three keys or an art piece that contains a labyrinth, as both are sacred to her. To begin working with her, go to a place that has a crossroads, stand there, take some deep breaths, and say the following prayer:

Hekate, ageless goddess of witchcraft,
The keeper of keys and guide of all crossroads,
Thank you for helping me choose the right path at this time.
Thank you for guiding my soul to lead me forward.
May your keys open my guidance, connecting both my heart and
*   my third eye to my throat chakra.*
May I open my throat and speak wisdom and truth.
Blessed be.

SPELL
Releasing Fears

This spell is best done on a new moon. For this spell, you will need a small jar or similar container of dirt from a crossroads. Crossroads are liminal spaces and help us with all kinds of works of magic. If you don't feel comfortable getting some dirt from a crossroads, then potting soil or garden dirt will do. You will also need a black candle; if you can't find one, you can use red or white. Set up an altar with eight small smoky quartz crystals, the candle, the dirt, and anything else that feels symbolic of releasing your fears. Eight is your sacred number, as it represents infinity and strength. But if you don't have eight crystals, you can use four or just one. The items that symbolize releasing your fears don't have to be complicated. If you fear flying, for example, you could place a photo of where you would like to fly to. You will also need a lighter or matches and a safe place to burn your answers (such as a cauldron).

For this spell, you could call on and work with Hekate or another "dark" goddess, such as Kali, Lilith, or the Morrigan. If you choose to call upon Hekate, you may want to add three keys to your altar as a symbol for her.

Before the spell, prepare the altar and also take the time to answer the following questions in writing:

+ What is your biggest fear and why?
+ What are other fears or anxieties you have at this time?
+ What does your ego or personality gain from holding on to these fears? This question is tricky but dig deep. For example, a fear of flying keeps you "safe" on the ground.

On a new moon (or within three days of one), cast a circle of protection and stand or sit before your altar with your journal answers nearby. Call on Hekate or your chosen deity. Take some deep breaths and become present. Light your candle, hold your crystal(s), and say, "Thank you, mighty Hekate, goddess of witchcraft, crossroads, and the underworld, for joining me. Hekate, guide my journey to be free tonight. Thank you to my Spirit Crystal for aiding my journey. Thank you for drawing my fears and shadows from me. Thank you for making me brave and whole."

Hold the container of dirt to your heart space and say, "I will speak and breathe my fears into this dirt, releasing them from my body, mind, heart, soul, and spirit." Read your answers to the journal questions. Take a deep breath and gently blow all the fear into the dirt. Next, burn your answers (safely) and say, "These fears are no longer mine. They no longer have power over me. They no longer serve me. I am free." Then let the papers burn and cool. Add the ashes to your dirt. Place your Spirit Crystal(s) around or near the container of dirt to lend their energy. Close your circle and allow your candle to burn down.

The next day, release your dirt back to the crossroads or somewhere else but not on the land you live. Take the crystals you worked with and wash them in water, releasing the heaviness and fears they absorbed. We need ritual as humans to allow our minds to reset. This ritual may be repeated when new fears arise.

Your Plant Allies

As a medium, you will need to cleanse yourself and your space often. You will need to find herbs or incense that you feel work best for this type of magic. You will also need to find plants and herbs you find protective.

Copal is a powerful incense that comes in a variety of colors. Use copal to cleanse yourself, your space, and your altar tools. You can also burn copal in honor of any of the death deities, as it is sacred to them. Copal protects and adds love to any space in which it is burned.

Carnations are sacred to many deities and are used often on altars. You can use the dried petals in spellwork dedicated to your healing journey. Carnations are symbolic of strength and protection.

Elder trees and berries have old lore and were deeply appreciated by many ancestors for protective, healing, and banishing medicine. Elderberry syrup supports immune health and strength. Elder wands are used in exorcisms and banishing magic. For protection, hang elder over the door you use most to enter your home. Grow it in your yard to keep curses away.

Pines and evergreens are deeply revered by witches of all kinds. Stand under a pine tree and ask it to cleanse your aura and chakras. Use pine tinctures to cleanse your altar items and space. Drink pine needle tea to balance your hormones and strengthen your immune system.

Your Crystal Allies

Smoky quartz is your Spirit Crystal, but like all guides, it has a team that it works well with. The following are crystals that work best with your Spirit Crystal and will enrich your healing journey.

Jadeite is sacred to the Indigenous peoples of North and South America. It has a light green color that is similar to the sea. Jadeite is an excellent stone for you to keep on your altar or when journeying to Paititi. You can also offer it to any of the deities you work with and place the stone near their statue if you have one. This stone will help connect you deeper to your best life in ancient South America.

Obsidian is not a crystal but volcanic glass and comes in different colors and patterns. Any type of obsidian will be nice for you to have in your home. Obsidian will absorb negative energy while protecting your own energy and boundaries. Obsidian helps draw out your shadows. Wearing it, holding it, or sleeping with it near your bed or under your pillow will bring the shadows out from your psyche. Once the shadows are more upfront and present, it can then help you face and overcome your fears.

Black tourmaline, also known as schorl, is a powerhouse protector. It protects you from curses, negative spirits, and psychic attacks as well as electromagnetic fields (EMFs). Place a piece by your front door to keep your home shielded from unwanted energy and guests. Carry or wear a piece while around other people to protect your energy. Ask it to lend its energy to you while removing hitchhikers or other unwanted energy. In fact, you can buy it in the shape of a wand to help cut away negative energy from your body and being.

Hematite when raw is red but when tumbled takes on a beautiful silvery sheen. Many people wear hematite bracelets to help increase and improve blood circulation. But another great benefit is protection. It is a very grounding stone and helps give you courage when you need it. It will aid you in tracking down and facing your fears.

Your Spiritual Womb

As a medium, you may wonder why you are connected to so many aspects of death, yet the sacred womb of creation is also part of your healing. When we place those who have passed into the earthen ground through burial, we are releasing their bodies back to the womb of the Mother. The underworld is not a hell like in the Abrahamic teachings; it's a restful and fertile place. The underworld is a womb.

Your sacral chakra is where your spiritual womb exists, and everyone has a spiritual womb regardless of the anatomy of their physical body. This womb is the creation center of your body. When the womb is unhealthy, fears take root and begin to grow. The opposite of creation is death. Working with deities of death actually helps to heal your fears and release them from your womb. Every day, place your hands over this area of your body, making a diamond with your index fingers and thumbs touching. Point your index fingers down toward the earth. Take a deep breath into your sacral chakra and then say, "Fear doesn't belong here in my womb.

My womb is a home for creation. From this center I create a life of love and joy. Fear does not belong here. Fear does not belong here. And so it is."

Eight Is Infinity

Eight is your sacred number because when turned on its side, it becomes the symbol of infinity. As a healed medium, you know that the soul is infinite and death is just another stage in the life of a soul. Eight in the tarot represents Strength or Justice depending upon the deck. You are both strong and balanced in this world and beyond. Eight is also symbolic of making your own way or creating your own path. You are daring, unique, and truly special.

RITUAL
Healing Your Womb with Dance

Dancing is a sacred and ancient healing ritual. Our ancestors danced to celebrate, mourn, honor deities, and express their emotions. Your body holds emotions, thoughts, memories, and healing. Every time you heal something on a spiritual level, it must also pass through the realm of your body. Your body can hold stuck energy as well as old trauma. The more you heal on a spiritual path, the more your body goes through. It's common to feel ill after a spiritual awakening or healing. There is always a physical purging that accompanies such healings. Your spiritual womb, or sacral chakra, is associated with your hips. Your hips can store emotion and trauma. You likely have tight or stiff hips, lower back, or knees. Dance can help ease this imbalance.

Many people who are of this archetype can be very serious. This seriousness is not a fault, but it's something that needs to be balanced. Lacking spontaneity, joy, play, and fun can wear on you and leave you feeling older in your body than your actual age. Dancing is all about emotional expression and release. Dancing gets us into the flow of creation and life. Dancing can be used to raise power for rituals and spells as well. As part of your healing, dancing like nobody's watching is key. In fact, it's best if no one is watching so that you can really go for it.

For this activity, find music that makes you feel something. Tap into what it is you are feeling now and use that or find music for how you would like to feel. You can find New Age music, such as shamanic drumming, or use modern dance music—whatever makes you feel like moving. Warm up your body first with walking or stretching. Then begin to move your hips. Try a figure eight from Arabic or belly dance. Remember that your sacred number is eight, and this infinity move will open up your physical hips and bring healing to your spiritual womb as well.

Stand with your feet hip width apart. Make sure your knees are slightly bent and feet are flat on the floor. Punch or point your right hip to the right corner of the space you are in, round it back, and then punch your left hip forward and round it back until you are making a slow sort of jagged figure eight with your hips. Then tune into the music you have chosen and begin to smooth out the four points your hips are making until you are creating a real figure eight. Allow your hands and arms to move and sway with the music as well. Breathe deeply and close your eyes. Then begin to break the figure eight and move your hips however you wish. Dance until you feel content, then journal about your experience.

Continue to practice freeing stuck energy in your body through dance, and try yoga or other somatic releases that call to you. There are plenty of free YouTube tutorials that teach belly dance as well as yoga for the hips. Physical health is tied to spiritual health. Because you are a medium, you are connected to life after death. But dance can bring you to the present moment. Dance brings you into your body and helps you feel the aliveness of your body. Use dance daily as a form of meditative release as well as a way to tap into your emotional and physical feelings in the present moment.

Palmistry

Palmistry is really an art of reading energy and people. The hands have minor chakras in their palms that connect directly to the heart chakra. Holding someone's hand in your own connects you heart to heart. You can buy books or read online about the different finger shapes, lengths, and palm line meanings, but as a medium, you may not need this knowledge. You might be able to rely solely on your own intuition and wisdom. Holding someone's hand gives you direct access to their energy, and you may be able to discern a lot through this connection. All forms of divination will come easily to you as you heal, but palmistry will be one that you can excel at if you let yourself try.

Being a Healed Medium

As you can see from reading this chapter, being a healed medium does not require you to commune with those who have passed away. However, this may be something you are interested in. If this is so, continue using the exercises in this chapter to clear fears, hitchhikers, and old stuck energy to open yourself up to any potential gifts that want to arise. If you are not interested in this kind of communication, simply let your guides know this. Continue to heal yourself and free yourself of fears. You are a special soul that walks side by side with death, unafraid and whole. You are truly the gold.

Notes on Smoky Quartz

The following is a list that will help you go further on your path to becoming a medium. Use this list as a way to explore your archetype and create magic and rituals of your own.

+ *Important past life:* Paititi, the city of gold
+ *Deities associated with this crystal:* Archangel Azrael, Jaguar, Hekate, Santa Muerte, and Raven/Crow
+ *Plant allies:* copal, carnations, elder tree, and pine
+ *Crystal and stone allies:* jadeite, obsidian, black tourmaline, hematite, snowflake obsidian, and rainbow obsidian
+ *Divination tool:* palmistry
+ *Sacred number:* eight
+ *Direction:* west
+ *Element:* water
+ *Chakra:* sacral (spiritual womb)

Chapter Six
Rose Quartz: The Lover

Rose quartz exudes love, just like you do. In this lifetime, you may have developed a wall around your heart to protect it from hurt, but you are truly generous and deeply loving. In a past life, you lived in complete spiritual peace and harmony on the ancient island of Avalon. You lived in your feminine and had no issue giving and receiving love fully and freely. In this life, you will be able to bring balance to your heart once more. With the help of rose quartz, you can open your heart safely to not just giving love but receiving it too.

Your heart is so vast that you easily connect to the realm of the angels. In fact, it is likely that your soul originated in this realm. In this lifetime, the connection to Avalon and the angels can help bring you back to balance. As a healed lover, you can learn to be in your heart space and make all decisions from this place. You can learn to heal your heart and fill it up with self-love. To be a lover doesn't mean to give and not receive. A true lover loves themselves first, and this love fills them up so much they can share it with others. If a path of love gives you pause or resistance, know this is your ego. The ego rules with fear, which is devoid of love. Choose love and you will be healed.

In this chapter, we will focus on your healing. The tools provided here are intended to heal your heart and open it once again. This archetype was almost called the earth angel because you truly are an angel on this earth. In fact, you will rediscover your connection to the angelic realm as well as the healing place of Avalon. You will also be encouraged to journal as a practice for self-love. Other practices you will learn are sacred paths and meditations to fill your own inner well. Go forth, my little lover, and discover who you have always been.

Prayer for the Lover
My heart is vast and open.
I am free to be loved.
I am loved.
I am loving.
I am love.
Thank you, rose quartz, for reminding me of who I am in my heart.
I awaken my memories of Avalon.
And so it is.

Avalon Is Your Home

Avalon is an isle of women. It is a magical sanctuary for women to be witches and to worship the ancient goddesses. Living a lifetime in a matriarchal, goddess-centered society allowed you to be completely in your divine feminine. You could be open, receptive, and loving. Being in your feminine regardless of gender allows you to rest and live your life more like a body of water. You can flow, you can ebb, you can storm, or you can be still. Living in your feminine allows you to feel without having to judge or justify the feelings. It allows you to trust yourself, your body, and the Creator completely.

In the current patriarchal world, the dark, mysterious feminine has been feared and silenced. Logic and distrust have reigned, and the goddess has been lost or demonized. But you are here now as a lover to heal yourself and help rebalance the world. Being in your divine feminine and connecting to goddesses is what your soul craves. It doesn't matter if you identify as a woman in this lifetime or not because we all have both divine masculine and divine feminine energy within our spiritual bodies. But for the majority of society, the masculine is disproportionate to the feminine energy. Part of your healing journey is to balance your energy and allow yourself to rest in the feminine.

Number Nine and Angels

The Hermit is the ninth card of the tarot. And like the Hermit, you need time to go within and light your own lamp. Nine is also a number of completion in numerology. It represents a peaceful end to a cycle. Your sacred number nine also corresponds with how many choirs or types of angels there are.

+ *Guardian angels and angels:* There are many angels that are unknown by name to us. Within this sphere is your guardian angel, who reincarnates with you in every lifetime. They are always with you, and all you have to do to connect with them is ask to. You can eventually learn their name and even build an image of them in your mind. To connect with your guardian angle, say, "Thank you, my guardian angel, for being with me now and always. Thank you for your tender love and protection. Thank you, angel, for revealing yourself to me. Make your name and image known to me so I can better know you. Amen."

+ *Archangels:* Archangel Michael leads the choir of archangels, and each one of the archangels has other angels who connect with and work with them. You can start working with this choir by connecting with Archangel Chamuel later in this chapter.

+ *Principalities:* These are the angels who lead and "rule." They help guide spiritual leaders.

+ *Virtues:* Virtues are the angels that oversee larger beings such as land and countries.

+ *Powers:* Powers are the protectors who work hard to guide us toward peace.

+ *Dominions:* These are the angels who look over all the angels listed previously.

+ *Thrones:* Thrones are wheels of light as described in some spiritual texts. They are the chariots of light.

+ *Cherubim:* These are angels of the book of life or Akashic Records.

+ *Seraphim:* These angels are the burning ones. They have six wings and are the highest choir of angels.

Forgiveness Is the Key to Connecting with Angels

Forgiveness is the key that will unlock your heart. Freedom and true love are found through forgiveness. Working on forgiving yourself and others will open your heart to angelic love. Use the following as a daily prayer to guide you toward forgiveness:

Thank you, angels, for opening my heart to forgiveness.
May I recognize my ego and the ego in others for what it is.
May I see beyond the ego's grasp and free myself of guilt, shame,
*   resentment, and anger.*
May I turn my mind toward forgiveness now and always.
Amen.

Morgan le Fay

Morgan le Fay was and is the presiding goddess of Avalon. Avalon still exists within the hearts and minds of those who have lived there. Morgan le Fay is a triple goddess. A goddess who can be young and wild, act mothering and creating, or bring deathly wisdom. Her name translates into "sea of fate" or "fairies." She is deeply connected to the ocean and salt water. She, like many goddesses, has been villainized. She has been blamed for the demise of King Arthur, but we know that there are two sides to every tale.

To honor and connect with her, you can wear and place on your altar Celtic knots and symbols of the triple moon goddess. Morgan can appear as a warrior maiden, nurturing mother, and wise crone. You can also place symbols of the sea in her honor, such as salt, seashells, holed stones, and water. If you live near an ocean or another body of water, you can say the following prayer while gazing into the water to connect with and honor her. If you don't have access to natural water near you, then gazing into a bowl of water will do just fine.

Dearest Morgan,
Lady of the Fae,
Lady of Avalon,
Ancient and wise,
Thank you for being with me on my quest of love.

May I be free in this lifetime of the mist that shrouds my mind, heart, and soul.
May I be free to live a life in love and trust.
May I be free to open my heart and be brave in my love.
Thank you, dearest Morgan, for your guidance and protection.
And so it is.

RITUAL
Sacred Bath for Connecting to Morgan le Fay

A sacred bath is a ritual that you may find soothing and enjoy repeating often. If you don't have a bathtub, you can use a foot soak or take a longer shower. Set up your bathing area with a white or pink candle, some soothing or feminine music, and incense such as jasmine or rose, and cast a ritual circle. Into your bathtub place a tumbled piece of rose quartz, salt (Epsom is best but whatever you prefer), and whatever oils or bubble bath that makes you feel good. If you don't feel comfortable meditating in the bath, say the opening prayer and save the meditation for after.

Once you are in the bath, close your eyes and take some deep breaths. Place the rose quartz on your heart space or in your left hand. Call on Morgan le Fay. "I call upon Morgana. Ancient, wise, and loving like the Mother Ocean we all came from. I am ready to reconnect to my divine feminine. I am ready to remember my life in Avalon. I am ready to be a lover, whole and loved in this lifetime. I am open to your love and guidance, Morgan le Fay." Close your eyes and allow your consciousness to drift to Avalon.

Visualize, feel, and sense that you have washed ashore on Avalon. The isle is shrouded in mist, and you look down at your body to see you are dressed in the most beautiful white fabric, and it almost seems to glow. As you rest on the beach, Morgan approaches you. The mist parts around her form, and she glows as she glides toward you. You bow. She picks up your chin and smiles at you. She takes your hand and says, "Welcome home."

You follow her onto the isle, and she leads you to a quiet white temple surrounded by trees. At the temple, a priestess greets you by placing her forehead to yours. You connect third eye to third eye, and she says, "Welcome home." You look around the temple and see rose quartz, candles, and flowers. Morgan leaves and you are alone. This is your time to say prayers, make wishes, and speak your truth. Take your time and perform the ritual from your heart that you need at this moment. When you are done, the priestess appears again and says, "May it be so, thank the Lady of the Lake." You repeat after her and return to the here and now in your ritual bath.

When you get out of the bath, journal about your experience. Baths with salt are incredibly detoxifying, and they mimic the womb of Mother Ocean. Bathing with your rose quartz helps to turn your whole bath into the essence of rose quartz, allowing the healing to be amplified. A bath is slower and more restful than a shower. A shower is masculine in its invigoration and quickness. A bath is feminine in energy and magic. As a lover, taking a bath helps you to slow down and tune into your own needs. Once you have established a journey to Avalon, you can do so again and again to gain insights and healing. You don't always need to be in a bath to journey here, but it sure is cozy to do so.

Journal Pause

- Record what you can remember of the meditation.
- What did you see, sense, or feel about Avalon?
- What did Morgan look like?
- What flowers, trees, or colors did you notice in and near the temple?
- How else can you use your bathtub for magic?

Heart Chakra Healing

Oh, your sweet, precious heart. The heart chakra is your portal and is associated with both green and pink. Green is considered the color of your lower heart chakra and pink the color of the higher part of your heart chakra. Take your left hand and place it now on your heart center. Your left side is your receiving or feminine side. Placing your left hand on your heart tells your body that you are open to receive. While you have your hand placed here, breathe into your heart and envision it glowing strong with both green and pink. Do this exercise every day as a reminder to take care of yourself and to allow yourself to rest in your heart space.

RITUAL
Self-Gratitude Journaling

Gratitude journaling has been proven to make you more optimistic.[1] Our brains are wired to find fault and dwell on the negative. This programming allowed us to survive and cannot be removed from our reptilian brain. However, negative thinking and self-talk doesn't help us survive, and we definitely don't thrive when we constantly think negative or limiting thoughts about ourselves. As a lover, you are incredibly sensitive and very hard on yourself. Yes, you may have suffered heartbreak in this lifetime, but it is nothing compared to the daily heartbreak you turn on yourself.

Having a healthy body image or positive relationship with our image is a struggle for most people. The ego, which lives in that reptilian part of our mind, often berates us like an overprotective and sometimes abusive parent. The ego evolved to protect us. When the ego shames you and punishes you with hateful words, it is protecting you in the only way it knows how. But you are not your ego or your thoughts. You are not your mistakes, faults, or shortcomings. You are a soul in a body having an experience.

---

1. Feldman, "The Power of Journaling."

The ego is not something we can get rid of, but it is something we can become aware of and work toward overriding with our heart-centered higher self. One tool that can help flip the ego and its control is daily gratitude journaling about yourself. Yes, you are going to practice writing kind things about yourself daily. For many of you, this will be extremely difficult and almost painful. The ego can have such a tight grasp on lovers because it wants to protect your fragile heart by pushing everyone else away. The best way to push everyone away is to make yourself feel unworthy.

I encourage you to try this exercise for the next twenty-one days and observe the feelings that arise. When the ego laughs at you or questions who you think you are being so "arrogant," let it throw its tantrums, and continue the practice anyway.

Every day write a list of at least nine things you appreciate about yourself. Some days the list may focus on your body and its parts. For example, "I appreciate my heart for pumping my blood." You may find it easier to focus on the organs and their function when your ego is being extra strong. But on other days, your list might include attributes of personality or physical appearance, such as "I am grateful for my smile. I am grateful for my generosity." Allow yourself to love yourself. Allow yourself to see your worth.

MEDITATION
Filling the Well of Your Heart

You are so very loving, even when you are closed off to others. Because of your big, wide-open heart chakra, you can become easily depleted and drained. This meditation helps you to fill your own spiritual cup and recharge. For this meditation, it would be best if you could lie on your back with a rose quartz placed upon your heart chakra (middle of chest). If not, hold one in your left hand. Take a moment to get comfortable, close your eyes, and take some deep breaths, filling your belly like a balloon and slowly exhaling in an audible way. In other words, take deep breaths with long sighs.

Once you feel relaxed, visualize yourself standing in a misty forest. The forest is lush and green. There is a gentle mist clinging to the trees and shrouding the path ahead. But you know you are safe. You begin to walk along the winding path through the trees and into the mist. The path seems to run along a creek, and though you cannot see it, you can hear it babbling. As you walk, you feel pulled by your heart. Your heart recognizes this place and is leading you down the path. Now you can see a clearing through the mist. The path ends at this clearing and here the fog lifts. You can see this clearing is surrounded by trees and the creek is running toward your left. You can see it just beyond the trees. Notice a beautiful stone well in the middle of the clearing. Approach the well. As you get closer, you begin to feel an excitement from your heart.

Once you are close enough, you lean both hands onto the well and look into the depths. The well seems to be endless, and the water is dark and calm. But the water is far below the surface. Know that this well is a symbol for your precious heart. The well is not dry, but it is not full. You notice a wooden bucket at your feet. And you remember the creek running near you. Pick up the bucket and walk away from the well, through the trees, and to the creek.

The creek is glistening in the sunshine. You can see rainbows dancing around it and beautiful smooth stones. Kneel at the creek and ask permission to take some of its water to fill your well. Listen as the Spirit of the Creek says, "Of course you may take the waters. These waters are ever infinite, as they belong to the Creator." Fill up your bucket, walk back to your well, and pour the water in. You do this process, not tiring but feeling more and more energetic as you go, until your well is filled, until you can gaze into the water and see your own reflection dancing upon the top.

As you pull your gaze away from the well, you notice a group of fae fluttering nearby. They are dancing and joyful. One approaches you because it has a message for you. Listen, feel, or see the message. Thank the fae. Thank the well, thank the space, but most of all, thank your precious heart. You begin to walk back to the path you started on, and the fog rolls in once more, hiding your secret well. Continue to walk until you are here and now in this body. Take a moment to stretch your body and then journal about your experience.

As a healing lover, you may need to return to this meditation monthly, weekly, or even daily to nourish and fill your own well. You are a natural giver, and this meditation helps replenish all the love and emotional support you give to others.

Journal Pause

- What does it mean to fill your own cup or well?
- What hobbies, activities, or habits fill your well?
- What people or pets help to fill this well?

Archangel Chamuel

Archangel Chamuel and his partner, Archaea Charity, are angels of deep love. Their energy is of soft reds and pinks. Chamuel is great to call on to heal any issues you have with love, whether it be giving or receiving it. He can help you rebalance your heart chakra and clear ties, binds, or blocks that you have here. Angels are multidimensional beings. Never feel like an inconvenience or undeserving of prayers or connections with an angel. They transcend time and space and can be anywhere and everywhere all at once, so your prayers to them do not take energy from another person's prayers. You are deserving of love and connection. You can use the following prayer to connect to Archangel Chamuel. Place your left hand on your heart and speak to him from this sacred part of your body and being.

Dearest Archangel Chamuel, angel of the heart,
Thank you for wrapping me in your white and pink light,
Keeping me safe and secure.
Chamuel, be my wings when I am afraid.
Open my heart to receive the love that is my birthright.
Guide me to allow love into my life.

Infuse me with the holiness of love.
May I truly know agape—the love for everyone.
Amen.

Your Plant Allies

The following are plant allies that will help you on your healing journey to embody the archetype of a lover.

Roses are sacred to Archangel Chamuel as well as Mother Mary and Our Lady of Guadalupe. All of these beings are embodiments of love and forgiveness. Keep roses on your altar to remind yourself that you are loved. Use rose petals in your baths and spells to bring love in. Wear rose-scented oils to remind yourself that you are worthy of love and romance.

Rosemary is a beautiful herb that can be used in flower arrangements, utilized in cooking, or drank as a tea. It also smells amazing when added with rose or jasmine essential oil. Rosemary opens the mind up to the present moment and helps to increase memory retention. Use it fresh to help you sleep and lift your mood. Burn dried rosemary to cleanse and protect yourself and your space.

Jasmine is a heady, romantic-smelling flower. Drink it in tea to remind yourself of your own ability to be loving and loved. Wear it to attract spiritual or higher love into your life. Burn jasmine incense before sleep for prophetic dreams. Use dried jasmine flowers in spells for abundance.

Birch trees are said to have brought humans language, as their bark looks like it has runes etched upon it. Use its branches to make a besom, or broom, to cleanse and protect your space. Leave milk or honey near a birch tree as an offering for good neighbors (fairies).

Apples reveal an inner pentagram when cut in half horizontally. Use apples for both protection and love healings. Wear or burn apple blossom scents to bring love into your life. Make a wand out of an apple branch and use it in spellwork to open and heal your heart. Apple blossoms are great in magic to encourage self-love. The scent will be healing to you and your heart.

Your Crystal Allies

Rose quartz is your Spirit Crystal, and it is true that it is the only crystal you truly need to evolve on your journey. However, rose quartz has connections to other crystals and stones that will only add to the love. The following are crystals that work best with your Spirit Crystal and will enrich your healing journey.

Holed stones, also known as hag stones, have a deep lore. They are associated with the divine feminine and goddess energy. The hole is seen as a portal that can help you see faeries. Holed stones can be worn or hung in your home for protection. Keep one in your hands or near you while meditating to invite a fae presence. You can place them on altars in the name of goddesses as a sign of devotion.

Watermelon tourmaline is a bit more pricey than other colors of tourmaline, but its unique coloring of pink and green makes it the greatest heart chakra healer. Remember that you only need a small piece, and the investment in such a powerhouse crystal is worth it. Place it on your heart center while meditating, and keep it in a place of honor on your altar when not using it.

Moonstone is a pearly crystal sacred to the divine feminine and moon goddesses. It is also sacred to Archangel Haniel. Having moonstone with you will help you step into your divine feminine. Place it in your baths, sleep with it under your pillow, and hold it while you pray. Moonstone is a crystal that really likes a good full moon bath to recharge.

Turquoise is a stone of love. It's a healer of the mind, body, and spirit. Place it on the chakras to heal and open them up to love. It is also protective and will help you open yet guard your heart. It works with the subtle energy of your body and has a deeply calming effect. Long ago, I was told that it doesn't respond well to being near or working with lapis lazuli.

Rhodochrosite is a pink or orange stone that is inexpensive and readily available. Despite being so common, it is powerful. It helps to reignite your passions. If you have suffered abuse or experience other trauma, it can help heal you as you work through these issues in therapy. Keep it with you during these sessions or while having a heartfelt chat with a friend.

Kunzite is a darker pink than rose quartz and is another heart opener. But it is more joyous than the other crystals mentioned. It opens the heart to joy and happiness and helps invite a lightheartedness. It makes a wonderful companion to any inner-child or inner-teen healing you are working through.

SPELL
Heart Chakra Anointing Oil

Daily ritual allows us to add magic to our lives. It also helps create a habit of self-love. You will create an oil to anoint your heart daily. This ritual will bring your precious heart to the forefront and focus of each and every day. This will become a daily act of love.

For this spell, you will need a roller bottle, a carrier oil (something light without a scent) and any combination of essential oils, herbs, and crystals you would like to add. If you can find chipped or rose quartz beads to add to the bottle, this would be ideal. For the herbs and oils, consider smells that evoke feelings of comfort and love for you. Some ideas are roses, rosemary, myrrh, jasmine, vanilla, patchouli, cinnamon, and sweet orange. You will need a candle (red or pink is best) and a lighter or match. To your altar, you can add some fresh roses or dried rose petals and small pieces of rose quartz to create an oval around your oil ingredients. This spell is best done, if possible, right after the Filling the Well of Your Heart meditation.

Before you cast a circle and light your candle, have all of your ingredients and your container to put them in. You may want to put on music that makes you feel content or that evokes a sense of comfort. Invite your preferred deities and guides into your circle and call on Archangel Chamuel to join you. "Thank you, Arcangel Chamuel, for being with me at this time. Today I step into my birthright to be loved, feel love, give love, and know love." Place your hands over the ingredients and say, "Full of love for myself and gratitude for all that I am, I create an oil that will remind me that I am loved, loving, and love."

Then with intention, create your oil. Begin with your bottle filled with whatever little bits of herbs and chipped crystals you wanted to add. Then fill the bottle about three-fourths of the way with a carrier oil. Next, add one to three drops of each of the essential oils you have chosen to use. Then give the bottle a shake and a sniff. If it's not smelling the way you would like, continue to add more drops of essential oil until you are happy. Please note that some people are very sensitive to essential oils, and you should test a bit on your wrist before wearing it daily. Please also do research on your essential oils, as some can make your skin sensitive to sunlight.

When you are done, hold the bottle to your heart and say, "Thank you to my Spirit Crystal. With your help I charge this oil with the remembrance of love. As I wear it, as I smell it, as I see it, I will allow my heart to heal and open wide. I trust in my angels and guides to protect my precious heart. I allow comfort and reception into my life. I am open to receiving love in expected and unexpected ways." Then give the bottle a little kiss if you feel so inclined.

Open the bottle and rub a little on your heart space and anywhere else that feels right. When you are ready, thank your helpers, close your circle, and journal about your experience. Finally, apply the oil everyday, morning and evening. Allow the oil to be a reminder of who you are at your core: a lover. You can say a prayer each time you place it on your skin, or you can just make it part of your daily ritual. When the oil runs out, feel free to do this all over again with different scents and different words.

Pendulum

Using a pendulum is a form of dowsing. Dowsing has been used by many cultures for thousands of years to find water sources, precious gems, and even ghosts. A pendulum can be made or purchased but is essentially a weight at the end of a chain or string. Finding or creating a pendulum with a rose quartz as its weight would be ideal for you. After you choose your pendulum, cleanse and activate it. Try using your left hand with your pendulum, as that is your receiving hand. Pendulums give direct yes or no answers and therefore make some people uncomfortable. But as you heal your heart and connect deeper to who you truly are, you will be able to discern messages that go beyond yes or no but also the why. Allow yourself to experiment with this form of divination and ask your angels to guide you.

You are a lover. You truly are love. Your angelic frequency connects you easily with all the angels and fairies. The angels want to help you, but they abide by the law of free will. You need not do any of this healing alone; call on the angels to assist you. If you are able to plant roses or keep a miniature rose in a container on your altar, do so. Roses hold such a high angelic frequency and are sacred to Magadelenes as well as the priestesses of Avalon. Allow yourself to open like a rose bloom in your own life.

Notes on Rose Quartz

The following is a list that will help you go further on your path to becoming a healed lover. Use this list as a way to explore your archetype and create magic and rituals of your own.

- *Important past life*: Avalon
- *Deities associated with this crystal*: Archangel Chamuel, Hummingbird, Butterfly, Morgan La fae, goddesses, all fairies and angels
- *Plant allies*: roses, rosemary, jasmine, birch tree, and apples
- *Crystal and stone allies*: any holed stone, watermelon tourmaline, moonstone, rhodochrosite, and turquoise
- *Divination tool*: pendulum
- *Sacred number*: nine
- *Direction*: north
- *Element*: deep earth (below ground)
- *Chakra*: heart

Chapter Seven
Clear Quartz: The Healer

Clear quartz chose you for a purpose. In a past life, you were someone who studied and spent much of their time helping to heal and counsel others. You performed healing ceremonies where you used your clear quartz to draw out the negative entities and energy from others and the land. You lived a life in Lemuria, or Mu. Here you worked with the quartz, encoding them with messages and planting them in the ground to make giant grids of healing and records. You saw the quartz as living beings and understood their deepest mysteries. You knew of the crystal's great power and how to wield it lovingly. In this life, clear quartz has returned to help you call back your power as a healer, step into it, and keep it.

Quartz connects soul to soul with you and sees your potential in this lifetime to be a healed healer. In ancestral cultures, the medicine person, midwife, or healer often went through a terrible illness, accident, or psychotic break before stepping into their healing abilities. They were "broken," and this began their own hero's journey into healing. Like a piece of pottery repaired in the kintsugi way, their flaws and struggles made them more valuable. You have overcome much in your lifetime. You are not just a survivor but a healer. Your healing journey will be accelerated and aided by your quartz ally. Quartz magnifies all healing and works with all chakras. Quartz removes negative energy, entities, psychic daggers, and past-life traumas.

In this chapter you will be given the tools that will amplify your own healing journey. You will learn how to protect yourself spiritually because this is essential to your overall well-being. You will learn to clear your chakras of ties and unwanted energies, freeing you to heal deeper. You will also learn how to enter and read the Akashic Records for yourself and others, bringing back messages of healing. Finally, you will make a special bundle that dedicates yourself to your path of healing. Your healing began when you picked up this book. Read on to gather your tools and evolve.

Prayer for the Healer
Quartz, thank you for finding me in this lifetime.
Thank you for giving me clarity to see beyond my own ego.
Thank you for awakening my lessons and memories of Lemuria.
I am evolving for my highest good.
I am a light.
And so it is.

What It Means to Be Lemurian

In Lemuria, you had a galactic origin, meaning you weren't fully human. You could be in water and breathe underwater, much like mermaids. Because of this, you have a strong affinity to water of all kinds. Both baths and showers are very healing for you. Take a moment, some time to meditate and pray in the rain, and you'll feel that connection. The rain will also help cleanse your chakras. Lemurians were earth and water stewards. They truly cared for Mother Earth and were a peaceful people.

Lemurians had a divine connection to clear quartz crystals. Quartz is like ocean water frozen into rock. Lemurians encoded the crystals with wisdom. It was like a form of Reiki; they would channel the energy into their bodies through their chakras and then into their hands. They would then plant the crystals into the earth. They were gridding the earth to help her evolution. This was a ceremonial work that all Lemurians took part in. Their favorite gridding shape was that of a spiral. Creating a spiral grid of clear quartz crystals on your altar can be very healing and familiar for your soul.

RITUAL
Daily Spiritual Protection

People with clear quartz as their ally need ritual in their lives. You will benefit from a morning and evening routine that takes you out of the mundane, 3D world and into the 5D or Spirit Realm. As a Lemurian soul, your frequency is high, and you often attract entities and other undesirables into your auric field. It's important to cleanse your chakras often and make sure you are placing spiritual protection around yourself daily. You need to protect your energy. You naturally heal the earth and those around you just by being here. This connection allows you to heal others and the earth without even realizing it. You can become easily drained if you aren't protecting your energy, as some people and entities may want to take more than their share from you.

Upon waking up in the morning, hold on to a piece of clear quartz at your heart and say the following: "Thank you, Spirit Crystal, for clearing my auric field, chakras, mind, body, and soul of any entities or energies that are not mine. Thank you for clearing away psychic cords and daggers. Thank you for connecting to me through my aura and strengthening my protection. May my aura be protected by your strong crystalline energy, not allowing anyone or anything into my field. And so it is." Take the quartz from your heart and draw it above your head as high as your arms can reach, then bring it back down to your heart again. You are using the quartz as a conduit to engage your eighth chakra to protect you. The eighth chakra is also known as a wiracocha, or soul star chakra, and is essentially the halo of light that connects to Spirit and protects you. Visualize a crystalline rainbow field encompassing you like an egg.

It's important when giving yourself daily protection that you ask your quartz to clear away all that is no longer serving your energy first before sealing you into its protection. This method will help ensure that you don't seal things into your field with you. You can practice this protection both morning and evening. In the evening before bed, this ritual will allow you to be safe while you wander in the dreamworld. Many of us travel in the astral realm into past lives and elsewhere as we dream. Especially as a healer, you most likely are healing other people and places in your dreams. If you wake up tired, this is why.

Journal Pause

- How have you been spiritually protecting yourself?
- How do you feel after trying this ritual?

Archangel Michael

Archangel Michael is often depicted as defeating Lucifer. He is depicted in armor with a big, fiery sword, ready to cut down any evil he sees. He is associated with the color blue, and blue glass can be used to honor him. He is both a saint and the ruler of all the archangels, but he really gives big brother energy. He is fiercely loving and protective. He has a stronger presence at this time because he is helping us shift the energy of the earth for the better. He is considered the helper and friend to all lightworkers. A lightworker is anyone dedicated to becoming enlightened and uplifting themselves and humanity. You are a lightworker. To connect with Michael, try the following prayer:

Archangel Michael, divine leader of the angels,
He who resembles God,
He who defeated the darkness,
Friend of lightworkers,
Protector of all who call on him,
Thank you for being with me now.
Thank you for protecting me now and always.
Thank you for being my friend and guide in this world and beyond.
Amen.

RITUAL
Cleansing Your Chakras with Quartz

Everyone should cleanse and care for their chakras on a regular basis. However, your chakras are likely to be very open and larger than the average person's. This means that your chakras need consistent care. This ritual is best performed weekly or anytime you are feeling sluggish or out of sorts. Do this ritual after your daily spiritual protection. Stand or sit up tall, light a candle, and hold a piece of clear quartz in your dominant hand. If you can, use a piece of quartz with a pointed end or, even better, a double-terminated one (sharp on both ends) for this ritual; it will be stronger.

In this ritual, you will call on Archangel Michael to assist you. Archangel Michael is connected to clear quartz and all those who call that quartz their Spirit Crystal. Archangel Michael is not just from the Abrahamic religions but has a connection to Pleiadean starbeings and Lemuria. Archangel Michael is a fiercely loving angel who carries a fiery sword. This sword can cutaway and clear ties and negative entities that have attached to your chakras. In this ritual, your crystal is acting like an extension of his sword.

To begin, call on Archangel Michael and your Spirit Crystal to assist you. "Thank you, Archangel Michael, angel who is a gift from God. Angel of the heavens and stars. Angel, you can cut away cords, ties, and anything no longer serving my highest good. Thank you for assisting me in clearing my chakras." Take a moment to visualize Michael and his energy. I see him as blue, like Krishna and Kali. His energy is warm and comforting.

Take a few deep breaths and visualize your seven main chakras. See them as spinning wheels of energy and light about six inches in front of your body. Next, take the quartz in your hand and bring it to your root chakra. Say, "Thank you Michael and my Spirit Crystal for guiding this chakra cleanse. May my chakras be cleared of all that doesn't belong." Hold the quartz at your root chakra and visualize or feel it drawing out whatever doesn't belong. It may look like mud or gunk in your mind or feel sticky or hard in your body. Then repeat this process on the other six chakras. Take your time and breathe deeply. When you have reached the crown chakra, take the quartz and run it through the flame of the candle you lit (carefully) and visualize all the gunk it pulled from your chakras burning away, the fire cleansing the quartz. Allow this quartz to sit in the sun for at least an hour to recharge.

Journal Pause

- Practice the daily protection and the cleansing of your chakras exercises for one week, then journal about differences in your energy, attitude, emotional well-being, and sleep.
- How else can you ritualize your day?
- Where else can you bring quartz into your daily rituals (meditation, journaling, yoga, card pulling, chanting)?

Quartz Gives Clarity

Clear quartz does connect to all chakras but also rules the third eye chakra; therefore, you can use it to heal and evolve to have clear thinking. Eagle is associated with this crystal because it can soar so high that ancestors believed it could reach the sun and bring back messages. You have the potential to soar high and see the whole picture of your own life and the lives of others. This is a gift that requires training, but chances are you have already had moments of utter clarity and have just known what to do. You need only to trust in yourself and your connection to your Spirit Crystal to step into this gift.

Opening Your Third Eye

Lemurians had prominent third eyes that allowed them to connect with one another telepathically. You have always been highly sensitive and able to pick up on the subtleties of others. You are good at "reading" another person. If you don't feel this is true, then think back to your childhood and try to remember when you turned this power off. Your third eye, when healed, will allow you to connect with others, read the Akashic Records, and easily do other forms of divination and channeling.

Whenever you are having a hard time making a decision, place your Spirit Crystal on your third eye. It will amplify your ability to use the powers hidden within. If you find that your third eye is too open, then envision it like a door. Open that door when you are channeling or doing spiritual work and shut the door when you are done, leaving it just open a crack. Imagine it like a bedroom door that is slightly open at night, and you can see light coming from the hallway through the crack. This practice will help you control when you are receptive and ready and keep you from feeling drained from being open all the time.

RITUAL
Entering the Akashic Records

Your natural connection to quartz will enable you to read the records of the earth, your own records, and the records of others. These records are what many refer to as the Akashic Records. *The Akasha* is a term for "the ether." Ether, in many cultures, is referred to as a fifth element. Ether is our invisible energy— this is the element we are working with when we do any kind of energy work, such as chakra healing. Throughout many religions and cultures, there are references to the Akashic Records. The ancient Greeks referred to the realm of muses. In Buddhism, the third level of consciousness is called alaya. This level of consciousness is also referred to as root or store consciousness. This consciousness is always present, and once we can access it, we can reach mindfulness. The Akashic Records are all of these things.

Lemurians encoded quartz crystals with the records of their histories, both personal and universal. Holding any piece of quartz—not just the ones sold as Lemurian seeds or record keepers—will help you reconnect to these ancient grids and records. I was given this ritual to lead you into the records in a new way that is aligned with the quartz crystal.

To access the records, you will need at least one clear quartz. Four would be best. For this method, you can either sit or lie down. If you choose to sit, you will place a quartz on the crown of your head, one below your feet, and one in each hand. If you lay down, then place one quartz on your heart, one at your feet, and one in each hand. If you only have one quartz, then place that one in your left hand. Once you are settled, take a four-count breath. Inhale for a slow count of four, hold your breath for four, release for four, and hold no air for four. Repeat this method four times. When you feel calm, say the following prayer to open the records. You can open them for yourself, someone else (with permission), a place, a business, or even a pet.

To open:
I step into the quartz crystal grid,
Ancient and wise,
Thrumming with a pulse that is beyond this time, planet, or existence.
I open my heart, throat, third eye, and crown chakras to receive
    the information.
I call on the spirit of quartz.

I call on my galactic team.
I call on my ancient ancestry.
I call on the lords and masters of the records.

Thank you for connecting me into the grid and finding the path to
    (my, person's name, place, business, or pet's) records.
Thank you for allowing me entrance into (my, person's name, place,
    business, or pet's) records.
Thank you for opening (my, person's name, place, business, or pet's)
    book of all that ever was, is, and will be.

The records are now open.
The records are open.
The records are open.
Now the records are open.

I see, hear, and feel clearly.
I see, hear, and feel clearly.
I see, hear, and feel clearly.
I see, hear, and feel clearly.

Once you say the prayer, envision yourself in a grid of clear quartz crystals. Then ask your questions of the records. I like to ask, "What do I need to know at this time?" The records are not a place for yes-or-no or binary questions but a place for deeper questions about the past, present, and future. Your answers will arise in a way that works for you. Remember which clair-sense you feel is strongest for you. Your answers will most likely come through the sense that is the most dominant. You may hear them (in this case, have your phone or other device ready to record your voice), you may feel them in your body, you might see them (again record what you see), or you might prefer to have a pen and paper to draw or write what you receive.

No matter what happens in the records, you are receiving. It just takes some practice to discern how you are receiving information. When I first began, I thought I would see, but I spoke instead. It was El Morya who came to me and told me to open my mouth. When I channel in the records, I am not conscious of what I am about to say, so I use my phone to record what is channeled, but it took me weeks of practice to discover this method. For some of you, the first time you try this, you will receive answers, but many others will need practice. If this is the case, open the records every day for twenty-one days, or until you receive a message.

Once you feel you have received the messages, you will need to close the records. Don't skip this step, as it closes the energy and shows respect for the process. Use the following closing prayer.

For closing:
I give gratitude to the crystal grid and all of the clear quartz that is, ever was, and will be.
I give thanks to my highest soul self for entering the records.
I give gratitude to the masters and guides of the records.

I unplug myself from the crystal grid.
I close my crown, third eye, throat, and heart chakras but not fully.
I am grounded in the here and now.

The records are now closed.
The records are closed.
The records are closed.
The records are closed.
And so it is.

When you are saying you are closing your crown, third eye, throat, and heart chakras but not fully, visualize or feel this like leaving the door to each one cracked open, not shut completely. When you are done exploring the records, it's important to close the records and do something grounding, such as having a snack or going outside. You may also want to place the quartz you used for this in the sunlight for at least half an hour to help them recharge. Make sure to record your experience in a journal, even if you didn't receive an answer. Also be mindful of the answer appearing later as a sign or a dream.

Journal Pause

- Have you ever had an Akashic Records reading done or have done one for someone else? If so, how did this experience differ?
- What did you see, hear, sense, or feel in the records?
- How might you use the ability to enter the Akashic Records in the future?

Healing as a Journey

Healing is personal. Using your daily rituals will allow you to begin to cleanse and heal your chakras and energy. Entering the records will allow you to heal past-life trauma and release yourself from old hurts, contracts, and lessons. Healing is a process, and as you do this work and continue to meditate with your Spirit Crystal, you will learn your own ways and methods of healing. You are invited to step into a place where you trust yourself and your crystal to work together to make you whole.

Your Plant Allies

For you, the mint family of plants, Lamiaceae, holds a special and sacred magic. Peppermint, spearmint, and mint make a great tea for you to drink before meditations or Akashic Record readings. Mint is both calming and stimulating, allowing a balanced energy. Use mint essential oils in spellwork to give the workings extra power. Wear mint-scented oils or perfumes for protection and overall health. Burn dried mint to cleanse and clear yourself and your space. Drink lemon balm tea for overall immune health and hormone balancing. Catnip makes a great tea for when you are feeling anxious or out of balance.

Redwood trees are Lemurian in origin. They are not of this world as we know it. When communing with them, you can feel their otherworldly energy and wisdom. If it's available for you to one day take a pilgrimage to the redwood trees, you will find a sense of renewed energy, and your Lemurian life will come into focus. It is illegal to take seeds from the redwood forests, but you can find ethically sourced seeds for sale online to keep on your altar.

Your Crystal Allies

Clear quartz is a true powerhouse of magic and healing. But it is really like a mother crystal that amplifies the magic of any other stone or crystal. The following are some of the crystals that work best with your archetype and will enrich your healing journey.

Lapis lazuli looks like a piece of blue kintsugi pottery. It is this deep blue with golden veins or flecks. Lapis lazuli helps open and heal your third eye. While meditating or entering the Akashic Records, place a tumbled piece on your third eye and rub gently in upward sweeping motions toward your hairline. My first crystal teacher told me that lapis lazuli and turquoise cancel out the energy of each other, so I always keep them separate.

Celestite is such an ethereal and healing crystal. It instantly raises your vibration and allows you to connect easier to your angels and guides. It helps to stimulate and open your clair senses and brings a sense of love and calm. It's truly the crystal for a spiritual healer or leader. Keep it with you as you meditate, journal, or do other healing work.

Selenite is a cleansing crystal. It is self-cleansing and doesn't need to ever be cleansed. It can also cleanse other crystals, as well as other ritual objects. It cannot get wet and doesn't need to go into the sun to recharge. Selenite does like some full moon light from time to time, though. It's a wonderful crystal to have as a wand to help cleanse your energy and cut away anything that is no longer serving you. You can use this wand to cleanse your home or any other space you wish. You can also cleanse other crystals with selenite. Selenite is very grounding and is nice to have placed in high-traffic areas of the home, such as the living room, or in an office.

Kyanite, like clear quartz, is an amplifier of energy. It will help you connect with your angels and guides. Like selenite, it doesn't hold on to energy, so it doesn't need cleansing. It makes a great meditation companion, as it is both calming and restorative. Many healers have prophetic or lucid dreams; kyanite will help to amplify your dream recall when placed near your bed.

Salt is a mineral, but it is mentioned here as a helpful ally. Salt is protective and grounding. It connects you to the elements of earth and water, which are the most healing for a Lemurian soul. Place salt in windowsills (on the inside) to protect your home. Have salt lamps in your home to help remind yourself of the smell of the sea. Keep salt on your altar to remind you of your watery origins.

River or ocean stones smoothed by water make wonderful palm meditation stones for you. You can collect enough to warm in the sun and place on your body for healing. You can use them in grids to protect your home or give grounding to what you are manifesting.

The Number Four

The number four, your number, is sacred to many Indigenous cultures and shamans. There are four elements for us to work with and honor, four winds, and four directions. Connecting to the four elements and honoring them daily will be healing for you as a practice. The Emperor is the fourth card of the tarot. He represents a deep power that comes from a spiritual place. Four also represents balance and being grounded. You are balanced in your ability to speak with the Creator yet remain on Mother Earth. You are grounded in your magical power.

Eagle Medicine

The eagle was considered by many ancestors to be the bird closest to the Creator because it could fly so high to the sun, even above storms. Eagle and birds of prey are sacred to you and offer you guidance. Study them, observe them, and connect with them in meditation. Eagle chooses whom he works with. To connect with Eagle, dedicate an altar facing east. Place upon this altar a depiction of him and symbols of air. You could use a bell, incense, or other items that make you think of the wind, birds, and flying. Then when you feel ready, face the east and say the following prayer:

Great Eagle,
King of all who fly,
Thank you for your wisdom.
Thank you for allowing me to see beyond fears and limitations.
Thank you for allowing me to soar above my ego and the mundane.
Thank you for allowing me to dream my own reality.
I wish to fly with you.
I wish to be under your wings and learn how to heal.
Aho!

RITUAL
Making a Spirit Crystal Bundle

In many Indigenous Native American cultures, medicine bundles are created for different purposes. There are personal bundles that are carried by the medicine woman or man. The contents vary in bundles, each one having its own special meaning to the individual who created it. There are pieces of cloth, animal bones, stones, and other symbolic contents. Bundles are often passed down through the generations. A bundle is a sacred possession and often carried with the individual. In hoodoo, conjure or mojo bags are created for spellwork and protection. In hoodoo, when a mojo bag is made, it is considered to be alive and must be fed. Many modern witches create spell jars for similar purposes.

Creating a Spirit Crystal Bundle will help you stay connected to your archetype. You are stepping into this power once again in this lifetime. Your bundle is a symbol of your evolution and Spirit. This is a personal journey, and therefore, your bundle will reflect your personality. Allow yourself to be creative here and play.

Bag: For your bundle, you will need a cloth or leather bag or pouch. This can be a drawstring bag that maybe you would put a deck of tarot cards in or a piece of cloth that you can fold and tie. It can even be a make-up bag. Whatever bag you choose, choose with intention. Reflect on color, texture, and symbolism. This bag is to be your bundle—it is like a small altar that you will carry with you.

Contents: A piece of clear quartz is essential, but what you place beyond that is up to you. You could add herbs, other stones or shells, beads, charms, sigils, a vial of water, salt, your hair—anything that feels magical or symbolic to your journey. As you grow and evolve in your spiritual journal, so will your bundle. Be mindful to open your bag at least once a month (full moon is best) to allow the contents to breathe, to let your crystal receive sunlight, and for you to reassess what you are carrying. You may also feel inclined to feed your bag with fresh herbs, cornmeal, or whatever else intuitively feels right to you.

Once you have assembled your bundle, create a ritual circle, call on whom you feel connected with, and hold the bag to your heart chakra (middle of chest). Take in several deep breaths and allow yourself to become present. Then say, "Thank you to the elementals and elements of earth, air, fire, and water for bearing witness to this rite. I call upon my Spirit Crystal for guiding me in all that I do here on this earth. May I be free to heal. Thank you to my Spirit Crystal for infusing this bundle with magic and amplifying its vibration. I unite myself with this Spirit Crystal Bundle. We are one and will travel this life together. I thank the vessel for being my companion. Like this bundle, I am a Spirit inside of a vessel. We are one. As above, so below. So blessed be." Then hold the bag above your head for a moment. Keep the bag with you as much as you can, and if you can't carry it around with you, then at least sleep with it under your pillow or lay it next to you.

You are meant to be a whole and healed healer. What you have gone through in this lifetime and before has prepared you for your sacred journey and soul lessons. Connect with your clear quartz and allow it to guide your path. Be open to understanding the past and how it affects your future. Connect with the mint family, as their herbal medicine benefits your body in many ways. Your sacred number is four, and it's important for you to connect with the four elements or four corners of the world daily. Eagle and birds of prey are sacred to you and offer you guidance. Study them, observe them, and connect with them in meditation.

Notes on Clear Quartz Crystal

The following is a list that will help you go further on your path to becoming a healer. Use this list as a way to explore your archetype and create magic and rituals of your own.

+ *Important past life:* Lemuria
+ *Deities associated with this crystal:* Archangel Michael, Oya, El Morya, White Eagle, Eagle, Thunderbird, and Hawk
+ *Plant allies:* redwood trees and members of the mint family: peppermint, spearmint, catnip, nettles, and lemon balm
+ *Crystal and stone allies:* lapis lazuli, salt, minerals, selenite, kyanite, and river stones
+ *Divination tool:* Akashic Records
+ *Sacred number:* four
+ *Direction:* east
+ *Element:* air
+ *Chakras:* third eye and all chakras

Chapter Eight
Citrine: The Manifestor

C itrine has been called the merchant's stone. Citrine chose you in this lifetime to help you remember your strong intuition and ability to manifest the life you desire. Citrine indicates a life lived in Atlantis, the technologically advanced empire that existed long ago. Atlantis fell because of a greed that overtook the society as a whole. As a people, Atlanteans forgot their spiritual ways and got lost in the sea. But here in this life, you can manifest from a place of love and balance.

Manifesting is attracting what you desire to you through prayer, ritual, actions, and spellwork. Citrine is here to help you remember your own power as a cocreator in this world. Your dreams can come true if they are aligned with both your higher self and your soul purpose. The key to being a healed manifestor is to honor and connect to Mother Earth. This rooted connection makes sure that what you are creating for yourself is in alignment with what is best for your soul and the soul of the earth. This balance is how you heal the heartbreak from your past in Atlantis.

Manifesting has become a worn-down, overused word. Much like the word *power*, it has collective negative connotations. Manifesting has been commercialized and tainted to excuse selfish behavior in some. A true manifestor does so from a place of power. This power is spiritual, balanced, and pure. You will be a natural manifestor when you are in a healed energy. To be balanced, you must reclaim your connection to the earth and the sun. You need to heal your root and solar plexus chakras. This healing will allow you to evolve on your spiritual path. Being an Atlantean soul means you have a natural connection to what others would call otherworldly or supernatural beings, such as dragons and unicorns. This connection proves that you bring magic to the mundane.

> **Prayer for the Manifestor**
> *I ground deeply into the mother below me.*
> *I am rooted strong.*
> *Thank you, citrine, for giving me balance.*
> *Thank you for awakening the lessons learned in Atlantis.*
> *I am balanced.*
> *I am abundant.*
> *I am whole.*
> *It is safe to be in my power.*
> *I am powerful.*
> *And so it is.*

Atlantis and Your Healing

Atlantis was an ancient, advanced civilization that was destroyed by a loss of spirit. The people became so far imbalanced in their masculine energy of taking that they lost their balance. A soul that has lived in Atlantis carries trauma. You are naturally a strong manifestor but are often blocked by your own fear of power and wealth. This fear is rooted in the Atlantean fall from balance. You may fear your own power and give it away without much thought. You may also feel strange about money. You may see it as an evil or feel it is an outdated form of trading.

But you can heal these wounds. Citrine brings you back to balance and helps remind you of your inner power to manifest. Citrine is here to blend with your own energy to offer a light to guide you. Your chakra that can be most powerful is your inner sun, or solar plexus chakra. Allow yourself to be a light again in this lifetime. Allow yourself to be cut free of karma from past incarnations. Become the manifestor that is your birthright.

Gaia: Healing the Mother Wound

Gaia is the Greek name for the soul of the earth. The earth indeed has a soul; all planets do. She is our mother, the mother that always will be there and will never leave us. Working with Gaia is healing for anyone who has ever felt neglected, rejected, abandoned, or traumatized by their own mother or mother figure. Gaia can soothe these wounds with her consistency and nourishment. As an Atlantean soul, you need to know that Mother Earth loves you and will not leave you. She allows you to heal any wounds in your feminine side. To honor her, make a conscious decision to help heal the earth with better choices on what you consume and throw into the trash. Do better for her and for yourself. To connect with Gaia, stand barefoot outside and say the following prayer:

Dearest Gaia, Mother Earth, Pachamama,
Thank you for nourishing me and holding me.
You are my mother forever and always,
The mother that cannot and never will abandon me,
The Great Mother who nourishes me.
Thank you, Mother, for protecting me,
Keeping me safe and fed.
Thank you for my home.
I connect deeply to you, Mother.
I am grounded.
I am safe.
Blessed be.

Journal Pause

- Do you see the earth as a mother?
- What is one step you can take to treat the earth better than you have been?
- Where in nature do you feel most at peace? Why?

Your Root Chakra

The root chakra is where we are tethered to Mother Earth. Anytime you feel anxious, worried, fearful, or ungrounded, you need to give some love to this chakra. The best way to do this is through practicing a grounding meditation.

MEDITATION
Daily Grounding

Grounding, also known as earthing, can be done in many ways. Those who are fortunate to live where they can walk in nature or be barefoot in the yard can ground this way. If you have a garden, tending to your garden can be grounding. Even tending to a house plant can give you this grounding energy. But on those days when you are indoors, use this meditation to help you connect to the earth through your root chakra to become centered.

Find a spot where you can stand comfortably (think mountain pose) or sit with your feet flat on the ground. Place your hands comfortably in your lap, holding your citrine in your right hand. Then close your eyes and take deep breaths into your belly. Try a box breath, breathing in for a count of four, holding for four, breathing out for four, and holding for four, and repeat. Keep taking deep breaths until you begin to feel like your breath has slowed and you feel calm.

Next, feel or visualize yourself surrounded in the light of your citrine. A golden light surrounds you from head to toe. Then call on Gaia to join you and help you feel grounded and safe in your body by saying, "Thank you, Mother Earth, Gaia, for helping me feel safe, connected, and present in my body." Take some more deep breaths, then say, "I am safe. I am grounded. I am present." Let your body relax, and continue to breathe deeply. When you are ready, open your eyes. Getting grounded is something you will need to do daily. Use this meditation or take a mindful walk outdoors. This practice is also helpful after any works of magic or divination to bring you back from Spirit and here in the present.

Archangel Uriel

Archangel Uriel is as if the sun gave birth to an angel. He shines so brightly and with so much love there is no room for fear when you call upon him. Working with angels is very healing, as they have not been human, so they only know love.

Call upon Uriel anytime you feel you need inspiration or illumination or feel like you are lacking in personal power. Use the following prayer to call on him, and if possible, light a candle in his honor beforehand:

Dearest Light of God,
Archangel Uriel,
You shine with the light of our sun.
Thank you for letting me step into your light.
Thank you for filling me with this light.
May I be inspired.
May I be illuminated.
May I be safe in my power.
May I be whole.
Amen.

Your Solar Plexus Chakra

Manipura is the name of the third chakra in your body and is the place of your personal power. This is the place of your gut feelings and intuition. You feel your intuition in your gut because of this chakra. Journal gut feelings that you have whenever they arise. This journaling will help you give validation to these insights and create a kind of communication between your gut and your brain. Take notice of when you feel butterflies or other tummy sensations. These feelings in your physical body are often correlated with your intuition and what you are sensing through your solar plexus chakra.

Journal Pause

- What does intuition feel like in your body?
- What does it mean to have a gut feeling?
- How can you honor your intuition more?

Your Crystal Allies

Citrine has allies in the crystal world that help strengthen its magic. The following are crystals that work best with your Spirit Crystal and will enrich your healing journey.

Golden healer quartz is a naturally yellow quartz. It is the crystal that will best help you recall your past life in Atlantis. Hold a piece in your hand or place it on your heart space while meditating or healing your past life.

Sunstone is a powerful healer of the solar plexus chakra. Place sunstone on this chakra while meditating to help open up and heal your place of personal power. Carry it with you when you need courage as a reminder of your inner sun and strength.

Tiger's eye brings balance to your life. It is grounding and protective and can be carried with you to encourage both aspects. It also has a subtle energy that helps you understand your own needs and the needs of others and find a balance between the two. Tiger's eye will help heal any issues you have of feeling worthy or deserving. It truly helps you step back into a place of personal power.

Pyrite is known as fool's gold, but it has nothing to do with fools. It is very healing of the solar plexus chakra and helps you discover your own inner gold. Keep it with you anytime you dive into self-healing work through prayer, meditation, journaling, chatting, or therapy. Pyrite placed on your altar will help remind you of the gold you have within.

Aquamarine is a powerful healing stone for Atlantean souls. It heals any fears of the ocean or other open waters that you may have. It connects you to the healing nature of the ocean and reopens your natural gifts as a manifestor. It puts you back into flow with your life and all that is. Wear it in jewelry or keep it with you daily to bring you back into balance.

Seashells are underrated healing tools. When collecting or buying shells, be sure that they are ethically sourced. Most shells that are sold are not. It's truly best to find your own or buy them secondhand. When finding your own, go for the broken or holed shells, as they no longer make a good home for a sea creature. Shells connect you to Mother Ocean and Mother Goddess. Working so much in healing your solar plexus chakra can leave you feeling more masculine than feminine. The seashells will help soften your energy. Use them in grids or place them around your home to remind you of your sacred origin.

MEDITATION
Soaking in the Sun

As an Atlantean soul, you struggle with power. Atlantis fell because of the abuse of power and greed that overwhelmed the people and the land. This past-life wound can show up as you being afraid of your own power in this lifetime. This meditation will help you step into your power in a healthy and spiritual way. Best practiced outside in the sunshine, this mediation can also be done indoors by a window. The solar plexus of your body, located above your navel, is your sun center. For this meditation, you can hold your citrine in one hand and a piece of either sunstone, tiger's eye, or pyrite in the other.

When you're ready, sit or stand with a tall spine. Place your hands and crystals on your solar plexus and breathe into this space. Imagine or sense your own sun shining inside of you. Feel your own warmth and your own power. You may see your inner sun as a many-petaled flower, a glowing mandala, or as a star. Visualize your yellow chakra glowing brighter and brighter. Let yourself see your sun and breathe into this space. Allow the heat of your hands to warm up your solar plexus.

When you're ready, say aloud, "I honor the sun. I allow the sun's rays to move through me and fill me up with light." Then imagine or feel the sun filling you with golden sunshine. See the sunlight entering your crown chakra, then moving down to your third eye, making both brighter and lighter. The sun fills up your throat and heart chakras, making them vibrant. Next, the sunlight travels down into your lower three chakras, making each one brighter and more vivid. The light fills up your chakras and spills over and around you, into your aura.

Hold this vision and say, "In the name of Archangel Uriel, I step into my power. I am no longer afraid to be the most powerful version of myself. It is safe to be in my power. I am powerful. I am powerful. I am powerful. And so it is." Now visualize your solar plexus growing brighter and bigger. Sit in your own sunlight for a while, and when you are ready, open your eyes and journal.

You can do this meditation every day for as long as it feels good to you. Anytime you feel your power slipping or you feel overwhelmed, stand outside in the sun and let it fill you up with heat and light. Allow the sun to recharge you. When people talk about light codes in spirituality, this is what they mean. Allowing the sun to fill you energetically can be a recharging and spiritual experience.

Journal Pause

- When, where, and to whom have you given your power away to?
- What does it feel like to give away your power?
- What does it mean to be powerful?
- What does it mean to stand in your power?
- Who is someone you think is in balanced spiritual power? Why?

Your Plant Allies

The following plant allies have the vibration that will help you heal on your journey to reclaiming your place as a manifestor.

Sunflowers move with the sun. They grow tall and lean their gorgeous blond heads to follow the sun. Sunflowers grant wishes, and their seeds help fertilize spellwork. Grow them as part of manifestation work. Keep them on your altar while working on staying in your power. Eat the seeds for overall immune health and hormone balancing.

Cinnamon is a powerhouse spice. You can find cinnamon or Ceylon cinnamon in your grocery store. Use it in protective spells. Blow it on your front door for luck. Burn it for cleansing and protection. Add it to warm beverages and drink it for protection and abundance. Bake with it for a lover to keep them enamored.

Nutmeg is another amazing spice. Sprinkle nutmeg on candles to add abundance, love, luck, and protection. If you are going to eat it, use it in small amounts because it can give you both hallucinations and an upset tummy in large amounts.

Basil can be used to bring in money and keep you protected. Burn dried basil to cleanse your space. Make basil tea to bring abundance into your being. Sprinkle basil in your wallet to attract more income. Tend to a basil plant on your altar to bring in abundance and protection. Scatter basil near your front door to bring in luck.

Citrus (all varieties) represent the sun. Dried disks of citrus can be used on your altar to represent the sun and your healing solar plexus. Make wreaths, ornaments, and pomanders during the winter months to keep you connected to the sun and its energy. Leave citrus on your altar for any deities you work with as an offering of abundance and health. Drink a glass of lemon water each morning to detoxify and hydrate your body.

Lady Nada

Lady Nada is the Atlantean form of Mary Magdalene. She is connected to pink roses, the heart chakra, and divine feminine wisdom. Being a manifestor, you are mainly healing your root and solar plexus chakras; however, Lady Nada will aid in healing and opening your heart chakra as well. The heart chakra is the portal or bridge from your upper to lower chakras. A healthy heart chakra means that the rest of your chakras can become better aligned. To connect with Lady Nada, place pink roses on your altar, place your hands over your heart space, and say the following prayer.

Lady Nada,
Mary Magdalene,
Priestess of Atlantis,
Thank you for opening my heart like a rose,
Allowing my heart to be a portal of healing.
Heal me of my past-life wounds.
Cut me free of old soul contracts and karma.
Help me be here now,
Free and safe,
Compassionate and kind,
Grounded and whole.
Blessed be.

Serapis Bey

Serapis Bey is an ascended master. *Ascended master* is a mainly spiritualist term for a person who has ascended reincarnation but is here as a master teacher to help other souls do the same. Serapis Bey is here to help you evolve and ascend into your soul self and purpose. He was an enlightened Atlantean priest who fled to Egypt to avoid the fall and destruction of Atlantis. He is here to help you heal any blocks that remain from your life in Atlantis. To connect with him, try the following prayer.

Serapis Bey, ancient and wise priest of Atlantis,
Thank you for coming to my side now.
Guide me into the crystalline ray.
Protect me as I ascend into the light.
Allow light to infuse my body.
May each and every particle of my being be infused with light.
May my chakras be filled with light.
May the light remove any darkness that lingers from this life or another.
I choose to be in balance.
I choose to manifest from love.
And so it is.

SPELL
Abundance Jar

Your past-life trauma from Atlantis created ties to negative beliefs about money and abundance. This can show up as feeling afraid you have too much or afraid you have too little. Shame is the result of both these feelings. Ritual can help heal these old wounds and free you of this shame. Abundance is your birthright.

For this spell, you will need a piece of citrine that you can keep in a jar for three months. You will also need a clean glass jar, an orange, a yellow or gold candle, three cloves, dried basil, a cinnamon stick, dried citrus or citrus oil, and sacred smoke for cleansing. You will also need a bag of sunflower seeds. These can be for eating or planting. This spell is best performed around a new moon.

Before your spell, set up an altar with all of your ingredients. Use sacred smoke to cleanse the jar, candle, crystal, and herbs. When you are ready, open sacred space, take some deep breaths, and become present. Light your candle and hold your citrine in your left hand. Call upon Lady Nada to guide you. "Lady Nada, priestess, healer of Atlantis, Magdalene, and guide of the heart, I call on you. Heal my heart of lack, greed, and any fears of money or abundance that I have, consciously or unconsciously. Remove from heart, soul, and spirit the woundings I have suffered from Atlantis, other past lives, and this life. Free me to be abundant. Free me to be generous. Free me to give and take without shame."

Next, hold the empty jar to your heart space and say, "As this jar is filled, so will be my heart. Let me see through the eyes of gratitude. Let me feel through the heart of abundance. Let me speak with the words of generosity." Carefully place your citrine into your jar, and one by one, place your other ingredients into the jar except for the seeds. For the sunflower seeds, hold each one to your lips and say, "I am abundant." Place at least seven seeds in your jar. You can add more if you want to. Once the seeds have been added, place your hands over your jar and say, "May it be so. I am abundant. And so it is." Place your jar on your altar, let your candle burn down, and close your sacred space.

Take a moment to answer these journal questions after this spell.

Journal Pause

- What does it mean to be abundant?
- How can you show generosity?
- What are ten things you are grateful for?

Leave your jar on your altar or somewhere else that you can see it daily. You can leave it for up to three months. When the three months is up, bury the herbs and seeds in your yard or somewhere else natural and cleanse your citrine.

Dragons and Unicorns

Dragons and unicorns are both real, but they are not in or of this earth at this time. Like angels and ascended masters, dragons and unicorns can be called upon to aid you in your spiritual evolution and journey. Dragons and unicorns are beings that exist in the same multidimensional place outside of space and time as other aspects of the Creator. At some point, both unicorns and dragons walked on this planet, but human error and cruelty forced them into an energetic realm instead of physical. This is why they both show up in myths and stories around the world. Just like you can connect to your Spirit Crystal, you can connect to dragons and unicorns.

MEDITATION
Connect with Your Dragon and Unicorn Guides

For this meditation, you will need to hold citrine to your heart and have an open mind. Begin by allowing yourself to be in a place of trust and openness. Allow yourself to remember the wonder and hope you may have felt as a child when you believed in the tooth fairy or some other childhood magic. The spiritual journey is more undoing and unraveling than anything else. Healing means accepting that what society and science tell us is the truth is only part of the whole picture. Atlantis was truly a magical place where what we consider to be supernatural or otherworldly was normalized. This is why you may have always been drawn to fantasy books or games as a young person. You may even recall fantastical dreams from childhood that may not have been dreams at all but past-life memories. So, allow yourself to step out of the constraints of this current incarnation and open to possibility.

When you are ready, close your eyes, and with your citrine at your heart space, take deep breaths until you feel relaxed. Call on your Spirit Crystal to be with you and guide you on this journey, "Thank you to my Spirit Crystal for guiding me and keeping me safe as I meet my dragon and unicorn guides and helpers of highest consciousness." Allow yourself to sink deeper into stillness and silence. Visualize or sense yourself floating in a liminal or in-between space. This place feels infinite and dark yet light at the same time. You are outside of the limits of both space and time. Know that you are safe. As you sit in this nowhere space, you feel something move below you and something move above you. Do not worry, as these beings will soon introduce themselves to you.

From below you, you feel an immense power and strength, and you know your dragon has come to you. Take a deep breath and invite your dragon to stand before you. As your dragon moves before you, take in their size, color, shape, features, and any symbols they may carry or wear. Take your time. Then when you are ready, ask your dragon for their name. Some dragons will give names and messages, while others will not yet. Dragons are fierce guardians and protectors. They protect you from lower energies and will keep you safe during any spiritual ritual or spell-work. Thank your dragon for showing themselves to you. Your dragon slowly glides to sit beneath your floating spirit self again.

Take a deep breath and invite your unicorn to join you. You can feel a power and lightness above your crown. There is a gentle yet strong magic here, and your unicorn begins to move down to stand in front of you. You feel a soft breeze on your face, and as you gaze upon your unicorn, notice their features, color, size, and anything else interesting about them. Be still and see if your unicorn has a name or message for you. Unicorns have a more subtle magic than dragons and are wonderful healers. They bring light into dark places and are good at expelling negativity and unwanted feelings or thoughts. You can call on your unicorn anytime you are working on healing yourself or others to aid you. Thank your unicorn for appearing and allow them to go back to be above your crown.

As you sit in this liminal space, allow yourself to feel the healing light above you that is your unicorn and the healing darkness below you that is your dragon. Sit in the healing a moment before returning to your body in this place, at this time. Once you return, take some deep breaths, journal about your experience, then eat some food or drink some water to become grounded again. If you didn't connect with either guide or only one, repeat this exercise at another time to try again. Sometimes these guides can be shy and need to know you truly are ready and willing to connect with them before they reveal themselves to you.

Once you have connected with both your unicorn and dragon, you can call upon them daily to protect you. Just visualize or sense the dark energy below you and the light energy above you. Dark energy doesn't mean bad. Dragons emit a radiance that is dark and almost seems to take the light from other things. This darkness is about protection and cloaking, not about evil. Thank your unicorn and dragon for protecting you and know they are with you. You may be able to find both a unicorn and a dragon carved out of citrine or another Spirit Crystal. If you feel so inclined, purchase these carvings in honor of your guides. If you decide to purchase a dragon crystal skull, see the last chapter on how to work with it.

Two

The High Priestess is the two card of the tarot. She represents someone who can be spiritual and in their divine feminine yet deeply powerful. You are this priest or priestess of ancient Atlantis reincarnated for a divine purpose. Two is representative of couples and love, balance, and finding a middle ground. As a healed manifestor, you are walking the line between the Creator and Mother Earth. You are to find the balance between above and below. On your altar, create a masculine/god side and feminine/goddess side. Allow the sides to have the same number of items and make them as balanced as you can. This altar will be symbolic of your own soul.

Astrology as Your Guide

Astrology is one of the most well-known forms of divination. It was used by Atlanteans to navigate day-to-day life. Step back into this energy and begin to understand the depths of astrology. Astrology is so much more than sun signs. There are different schools of thought and many minor aspects that people are still discovering. As a healed manifestor, you can use astrology to help be and feel empowered in your own life. You can draw power from knowing the energy of the cosmos and their effect on your day-to-day life. You can also better plan with astrology as your guide. Naturally good at math and with numbers, you will find that astrology and its patterns come easily to you.

Atlantis and Egypt Connection

It is of no coincidence that when heat is applied to a piece of amethyst it transforms into what looks like citrine. Amethyst is connected to ancient Egypt in the way citrine is connect to Atlantis. In astrology, one has their sun sign, but they also have an ascendent, or rising, sign. Think of amethyst as your rising Spirit Crystal. Atlantis and Egypt are closely related. Once you complete the healing in this chapter, move on to the chapter on becoming an alchemist.

Citrine is here to help you manifest the life you need. As you continue to work on your own evolution and healing, you will begin to better understand your place in the world. To manifest from a place of grounded love and balance is to make real magic. The key to manifesting is the balance of masculine and feminine, sun and earth. You are safe here in this lifetime to once again shine. You are safe to be in your power and to be happy. You deserve it.

Notes on Citrine

The following is a list that will help you go further on your path to becoming a manifestor. Use this list as a way to explore your archetype and create magic and rituals of your own.

+ *Important past life:* Atlantis
+ *Deities associated with this crystal:* Archangel Sandalphon, Archangel Uriel, Brigid, Whale, Dolphin, and Lady Nada
+ *Plant allies:* sunflower, cinnamon, clove, nutmeg, basil, and all citrus
+ *Crystal and stone allies:* golden healer quartz, red jasper, sunstone, tiger's eye, pyrite, aquamarine, and seashells
+ *Divination tool:* astrology
+ *Sacred number:* two
+ *Direction:* below
+ *Element:* earth (above ground)
+ *Chakras:* root and solar plexus

Chapter Nine
Amethyst: The Alchemist

Ancient Egypt is calling you. You lived a life in this ancient, advanced, and mysterious time and knew the powers of crystals. Amethyst has returned to you in this lifetime to offer a healing of balance. You are highly intelligent and tend to lead with your head, not your heart. Amethyst holds the strongest alchemy. Alchemy offers transmutation, not just transformation. Amethyst has the power to turn shadows into light and negatives into positives. Amethyst holds the power to release lower karmic energy, freeing you to evolve spiritually.

An amethyst connection indicates a tendency to need to see in order to believe. You are probably more skeptical than most who would read a book like this one. You enjoy logic, science, and have a fantastic memory. Your mind is where your power is manifesting at this time, but as you evolve and heal, you will be able to root this power into your heart and body for a more balanced approach to life. You often have divine inspiration but may not have always recognized it as such.

This chapter is dedicated to your reeducation in alchemy. You will learn foundational knowledge of alchemy so that you can continue this study as part of your healing journey. One of your healing tools is the use of the violet flame of transmutation. You will learn how to connect with and heal from this flame. You will also reconnect yourself with Isis and Thoth in order to open yourself back up to the magic you once knew in Egypt.

Prayer for the Alchemist
Thank you, Amethyst, for remembering me.
I step into alchemy in trust.
I call on the violet flame to burn away all that no longer serves me.
I am the violet flame.
The violet flame is me.
I am an alchemist.
I am the magic.
I am the gold.
As above, so below.

An Alchemist in Egypt

Amethyst's archetype is the alchemist. Alchemy originated in ancient Egypt. Alchemy is the magic of transmuting the mundane into something magical. Ancient Egypt was also known as Khem, which is the root of the word *alchemy*. An alchemist is not just any kind of magician but one who has gone through the seven stages of alchemy and liberated their very soul. You have been chosen in this lifetime to remember this role because it will serve as a reminder to your personal power and the importance of spiritual practice. Amethyst being your Spirit Crystal means you have immense power. This power may be something you have already remembered in dreams or have felt flashes of in this life.

The Twelve Gates of Alchemy

Alchemy is a large field of study, so for our purposes, we will begin with the twelve gates of alchemy. These gates, or rings on a spiral, are the same twelve phases that every person follows on their healing journey—whether they consider themselves to be an alchemist or not. Every person that chooses to heal and evolve spiritually embarks on a spiral journey after awakening. It's a spiral that goes inward and upward. As you progress on this journey, you go deeper within yourself but also higher to the Creator. The twelve stages are detailed briefly in the following section.

+ *Calcination:* This is the spiritual awakening. It is the moment you decided to pursue something different in hopes of a better understanding in this lifetime.

+ *Dissolution:* This represents the cleansing and clarity that comes with an awakening. Suddenly, you see the world and your place in it as different and with less limitations.

+ *Separation:* This is the stage of cutting cords, releasing old stories, and creating new boundaries.

+ *Conjunction:* After releasing what and who no longer serves you, this is the stage of empowerment and unmasking. This stage is when you feel comfortable to speak your truth and begin to understand your soul's mission.

+ *Putrefaction:* Shadows and fears rise, and you must face and integrate them in this stage. This is what others call the dark night of the soul. This is when all that has been denied or ignored rises to be healed. Shedding, purging, and decluttering of your mind, body, soul, and life are necessary.

+ *Coagulation:* You are becoming of a higher frequency and have shed much; you are stepping into who you are meant to be at a soul level. This is a stage of joy and comes as a break after the purging of the previous stage.

+ *Cibation:* Mindfulness practice comes in here to keep and maintain your newfound understanding and freedom. This stage is meditation, daily ritual, and spiritual devotion.

+ *Sublimation:* This stage is when all feels right in the world. You feel at one in your soul, mind, and body. It is another stage of joy and clarity of your mind, body, and soul connection.

+ *Fermentation:* Fermentation is slow aging. This is the practice of maintaining what you have healed and allowing wisdom to come. It is similar to cibation but the practices deepen.

+ *Exaltation:* This stage brings the pure ecstatic joy that comes with feeling like you are one with the Creator. You can manifest and all seems so clear and easy. You understand your soul's purpose and you begin to make changes to follow your destiny.

- *Multiplication:* This stage is why I explained this process to be more of a spiral than a straight path. Here you go back and repeat previous stages that are needed to further the process of ascension.

- *Projection:* You are you fully integrated as your soul self. You no longer have to wear any masks or speak untruths. Your frequency is high, and you are living your purpose.

As you embrace this path of alchemy once again in this lifetime, you will heal in the stages described above. Some of these stages will last minutes while others will last years. You will repeat some of the stages, but ultimately, you will find your inner gold. Amethyst is here to help you with every single stage. Amethyst is your true philosopher's stone helping you transmute yourself.

RITUAL
The Twelve Gates Journaling

You are evolving and growing constantly on your spiritual journey. It's important for you to take the time each week to have a check-in with yourself. Pick a day of the week and set aside about an hour of your time to go within, reflect, and write. Ritualize this to make it more powerful for your soul self. Light a candle and incense and have amethyst around and near you. You may even want to have a short meditation before journaling. You need ritual, and you need to set aside special time for yourself as part of your healing journey. Once you have shifted and have the time to sit and write, focus on the following questions, and as your ritual progresses, add your own questions.

1. Which of the twelve gates of alchemy have you recently entered? How do you know?

2. What does it feel like in your body to be at this gate in your healing spiral?

3. What is surfacing for you to address, heal, and transmute at this time?

4. What spiritual signs, ahas, lessons, dreams, synchronicities, or moments have you recognized this week?

5. When you really tune in with your own intuition, what do you hear, feel, see, or sense?

The Tarot

As an option, you can also use a deck of cards to go along with the previous journal questions to give you even more clarity. The origin of the tarot as we know it today is murky. But according to lore, on the god Ptah's altar in Memphis, images were found engraved in gold that resemble the major arcana of the tarot. Some believe that the tarot was an Egyptian book disguised as cards to escape burning, enabling the wisdom to survive. Others believe that Thoth is the true creator and author of the original tarot. You can even find a deck by that name created by Aleister Crowley.

The tarot can be a great tool, especially for an alchemist. It tells the story of a fool who journeys through life to become enlightened. He sheds his ego (Death card) and faces his addictions (Devil card) only to understand all there is to know (World card). The minor arcana cards are each tied to the four elements: earth, air, fire, and water, which are also important in alchemy. The tarot will be an ultimate tool for healing and divination for you as you step more and more into your true archetype. Choose a deck that you feel drawn to and begin to unlock its mysteries in your own way and in your own time. Keep an amethyst with your deck to heighten its connection to you and your highest self. Keep a deck for this special ritual with an amethyst on top to help bring even more clarity.

Archangel Zadkiel

Archangel Zadkiel is the angel of the violet flame. He has a purple energy and is deeply connected with amethyst crystals. He is an angel of mercy and aids any change, transformation, and transmutation you seek on your healing journey. To connect with him, hold your amethyst to your heart and say the following prayer:

Archangel Zadkiel, angel of the violet flame,
Angel of alchemy and transmutation,
Thank you for surrounding me in your violet light.

May it infuse me with the energy of mercy.
In forgiveness, I am free.
May I be free from lower karma.
May I be free of lower vibrations.
May I transmute and be whole again.
As above, so below.

MEDITATION
The Violet Flame

The violet flame can help you anytime you are stuck in some of the less desirable gates of alchemy. The spiral of healing is not always easy, and sometimes you can feel heavy with the burden of healing yourself. This is when you can turn to the practice of working with the violet flame. There are different colored flames that we can call on and use to help clear our energy, one for each color in the rainbow. For this meditation, we will call on the violet flame. The violet flame is associated with the amethyst crystal as well as Archangel Zadkiel. It's the flame that burns away lower karmic energy and can help lighten you in your mind, body, and soul. The violet flame clears your chakras as well as your auric field.

Before you begin, gather amethyst crystal(s). If you only have one, you will place it on your solar plexus chakra (between your ribs and navel). Otherwise, you will gather seven and place them on or near each of your seven chakras. Next, take your amethyst crystal and rub it in your hands back and forth until you feel a bit of heat. Do this with each crystal. For this meditation, it's best to lie down on your back, but I encourage you to do whatever feels right for your body. Take a few deep breaths to ground and say this prayer or one similar: "Thank you to my angels and guides for protecting me during this meditation. Thank you to my Spirit Crystal for lending your energy. I call on the aid of Archangel Zadkiel to guide me through this healing. Amen."

When you feel relaxed and ready, close your eyes. Visualize yourself in a safe place in nature. You are on a path in the forest, and in the distance, you can see a mountain. You walk toward the mountain feeling called. You are safe, and you feel angels and guides with you. You continue to walk, and as the mountain draws near, you can see a cave entrance. Next, you notice a violet light emitting from the cave. As you approach the cave, you see that Archangel Zadkiel is standing at the entrance. Observe him and take notice. Does he have wings? If so, what are they like? What kind of clothing does he wear? Any symbols on or near him? What color are his eyes? He smiles and welcomes you to the cave of the violet flame. He says that before you enter, you must open your chakras. You feel them opening and growing wider and larger.

You enter the cave. It is empty save for the violet light. The light is in front of you and is a huge egg-shaped, violet-purple flame. You know that it's safe for you to enter the flame. Feel yourself inside the violet flame. It is a big flame that doesn't burn or hurt you. It's violet in color, like an amethyst. But there are also hints and flecks of gold and rainbow. Hold on to this image as best you can, breathing in and out slowly.

When you are ready, say, "I allow the violet flame to engulf me. I allow it to burn away all that no longer serves me. I allow it to dissolve old karma, soul contracts, and cords. I invoke the violet flame. I am the violet flame. The violet flame is me. My path ahead is clear. I am whole. And so it is." Imagine the flame cleansing you and burning away all that is no longer serving you. Next say, "Thank you to my Spirit Crystal for connecting me to the violet flame and infusing my being with the alchemy I need at this time. As above, so below." Visualize the violet flame pouring energy and healing into your crown chakra. When you are done, thank Archangel Zadkiel and your Spirit Crystal and exit the flame. As you leave the cave, you feel your chakras return to their regular size. Now continue on the path you came from, returning to the here and now in your room and in your body. Journal about your experience.

Lady Isis

Isis, also known by Au Set, is a winged mother goddess of the Egyptian pantheon. There were many temples dedicated in her honor. She is a mother of the moon as well as a goddess of the underworld. To connect with her, dedicate an altar with a statue of her or symbols from ancient Egypt, such as a pyramid, scarab, or an ankh. You can find many images of her in oracle decks as well as New Age songs made in her honor. She is easy to connect with and rewarding to work with, as she truly is a loving mother goddess. To begin your connection with her, try the following prayer:

Isis Ma,
Lady Isis,
Our Mother from Egypt and the Stars,
Our Winged Mother of Creation,
Thank you for being with me again in this lifetime.
Help me to know my power once again.
Help me to see who I truly am.
Guide me to be whole.
As above, so below.

RITUAL
Calling Back Your Power

In order to reach the stages of alchemical conjunction and coagulation or beyond, you must be willing to step into your own power fully. No one can truly take all of your power. At times, we may give away the authority of our voice, body, mind, and even our heart, but your true power is always within you. An alchemist is a powerful magician. In this lifetime, you have consciously and unconsciously allowed your power to be diminished. You give away your power when you hide who you truly are, when you deny yourself joy or love, or when you don't speak your truth.

First, holding your amethyst crystal or having it near you, think about what it means to give away your authority or power. It may be in rejecting a compliment, not speaking up for fear of judgment, saying yes when you want to say no, being a victim of a crime, or any time you sacrificed your own comfort or happiness for another.

Now, list the times, places, people, and situations in which you gave away your power or felt powerless. If you aren't sure, this would be any time you felt like a victim or a martyr or gave into peer pressure.

Next, write a list taking the power back in the first person like this: "I take my power back. I take my power back in the name of my ancestors who gave it away. I take my power back from my mother. I take my power back from my father. I take my power back from the masculine energy. I take my power back from illness and sickness. I take my power back from fear." Write and write until you feel you have listed everyone and everything you can think of. You will use this list in the ritual.

In the following ritual, you will connect with the magic and power of Isis and Osiris.

Isis resurrected her beloved, Osiris, after he was murdered by Set. Isis and Osiris are called on in this ritual because you are playing both the role of Isis and Osiris. You are resurrecting yourself by calling back your power (Isis) but also being resurrected (Osiris).

When you are ready, cast a protective circle and light a purple, black, or white candle. Hold your amethyst to your third eye and then say, "I call on everlasting Isis and her partner, Osiris. Isis, who holds the power of resurrection, and Osiris, who was resurrected, guide me to take my power back so I can be forever in my power and unbound." Hold the amethyst in your left hand. Feel its power and draw the crystal to your heart. Then read your second list aloud. When you are done listing all the people, places, and times you want to take your power back from, say, "In the name of Isis, I am resurrected. I am resurrected. I am resurrected. Blessed be." If you wish, you may light your list on fire at the end (safely).

Take some deep breaths, thank the deities and your crystal, close your circle, and journal about your experience.

Channeling and Your Crown Chakra

The crown chakra is violet, just like your Spirit Crystal. In order to connect to your natural abilities to channel information directly from the Creator, place a piece of amethyst on your crown while praying and meditating. You may at times suffer from headaches, sinus pressure, or the feeling of brain fog or being ungrounded. When these feelings occur, it could mean that your crown chakra is too open or blocked. To help restore balance to this chakra, place a piece of amethyst on each of your seven main chakras. Use small tumbled stones and lie on your back, placing them on your body. Put on some violet flame music; there is a lot of free violet flame ambient meditation music available. Close your eyes and take deep breaths. Call on your Spirit Crystal to realign your chakras, "Thank you to my Spirit Crystal for aligning my chakras. May they be unblocked, healed, and neither too open nor too closed. Allow my energy to flow freely from root to crown unblocked. May I know peace in my body and mind. Amen." Then allow yourself to lay in meditation for at least fifteen minutes with the amethyst in place.

Your Crystal Allies

As an alchemist, you will be drawn to many crystals in your lifetime. The following are crystals that work best with your Spirit Crystal and will enrich your healing journey.

Moldavite is a rare crystal. Moldavite was formed when a meteorite crashed near the Moldau River in the Czech Republic. It is only found in this location. When purchasing this crystal, read reviews carefully and remember that a small piece will be enough for you to work with. It's extremely powerful and can make some people feel nauseated or dizzy at first. To adjust to its energy, wear or hold it for short meditations, then place it back on your altar to give yourself breaks. It connects you with galactic ascended masters and guides. It can help you recall your starseed origins and connect to a higher cosmic power. It is very delicate and fragile; cleanse it gently with water.

When polished, labradorite looks like the northern lights trapped under icy waters. Labradorite is known for its ability to help bring you to a higher version of yourself. It facilitates spiritual growth and transmutation. It is both calming and protective of your mind and energy. Keep it with you when meditating or doing any kind of spellwork, as it will help you transcend the space and time you are in. Gather a collection of small pieces to use in grid work, as they lend great energy and help accelerate spellwork.

All fluorites are wonderful for alchemy. They come in many colors and are a delicate crystal that doesn't like direct sunlight or salt. Fluorites are grounding, which is something you need on a daily basis. Place them around your home and wear them on your body to help keep you tethered to the earth. They are great crystals to have with you when you are learning something new. Look for the violet variety to keep with your Spirit Crystal, as their energy is symbiotic, and they will help strengthen each other.

RITUAL
Writing with Thoth

Once you have entered the alchemical stage of cibation and beyond, the maintenance of your healing becomes important to you. You need stability in your daily spiritual practices, as well as rituals to continue your evolution. It's important for you to write your own prayers, rituals, spells, and manifestations. You have a hard time following what others tell you to do in spirituality, and this is because you know the power of words. You need them to come from your heart with your intentions in order to work best for you.

Thoth (pronounced toth) is the Egyptian god with an ibis head. He is a god of writing and wisdom and was also known in other places as Hermes Trismegistus and Mercury. He is the god and writer of the infamous Emerald Tablet. This tablet is where we get the magical phrase "as above, so below" from. For this ritual, you will call on Thoth and your Spirit Crystal to guide your creation. You are essentially opening to channel your highest consciousness to create daily prayers, spells, and rituals.

For your daily prayers, you want to include asking for protection, sharing gratitude, and asking for guidance or assistance at this stage in your spiritual journey. Spiritual protection is important when living a magical life, as your magic can attract unwanted attachments. Daily gratitude will help to keep your frequency high and aid in your own inner alchemy. Finally, the angels, guides, and deities you choose to work with want to help you. They are just waiting for you to ask.

For this ritual, pick a day around a new or full moon to write your daily prayers for the month. When the next new or full moon approaches, you can use this process to change the focus and intentions of your prayers. Open sacred space, light a white or silver candle, and have a pen and paper ready and an amethyst with you.

First, take the amethyst and place it on your heart space and say, "Thank you to my Spirit Crystal for guiding my highest self to come forward and to be present here and now." Next, place the crystal in your writing hand and say, "Thank you to my Spirit Crystal for guiding my hand to write what is in my heart." Then put the amethyst on the crown of your head and say, "I thank my Spirit Crystal for connecting me to the mighty and wise Thoth. Thoth, mighty and wise creator of the Emerald Tablet, I open myself to your wisdom. I open myself to my own inner wisdom. I open myself to alchemy." Then take a deep breath and begin writing. Write whatever comes to mind, don't think about spelling or punctuation. Just write until you feel you have nothing else to write. Don't be surprised if you end up writing or drawing symbols as well. These sigils or talismans can be used as part of your daily practice and magic. When you are done, thank Thoth, your Spirit Crystal, the space, and your highest self and close your sacred space.

After you have closed your circle, read over what you have read. Edit it into the words you will use daily for this moon cycle. Look for advice, ideas, symbols, or other information that has been given to you. Draw out any symbols that have been given and place them on your altar with an amethyst on top to amplify the magic.

Your Plant Allies

The following plants offer the magic you need to continue your path of alchemy.

Lavender is not just a soothing and calming herb. It is a fierce protector. Grow it in your yard, drink it as a tea, wear it in an oil, and burn it to cleanse and protect yourself and your space. Use it in spells to aid in transmutation as well as banishing. Not only does it soothe and banish but it can also open your heart and bring in love. It is a great ally to have in your alchemy apothecary.

Myrrh is sacred to Isis. Burn myrrh incense or use myrrh oil when doing spellwork with her. Use the oil to anoint candles in her honor. It is also sacred to Ra and other Egyptian deities. As an incense, it is both purifying and uplifting.

Myrrh also increases the power of any other plant or herb ally, which is why you often find it with frankincense.

Oregano oil taken as a tincture or pill is a powerful antiviral and antibacterial (use with caution). Sprinkle oregano onto candles to banish unwanted energy, break curses, and encourage overall health. Plant oregano to bring love into your home and life.

Ginger in tea soothes a headache, stomachache, heartburn, and menstrual cramps. But this overall panacea also adds a fiery energy to spellwork. Sprinkle it on candles to add power to any kind of spell.

Figs are sacred to Isis. Lay them on her altar and eat them in her honor. Figs are used in fertility and abundance spellwork. Keep a fig branch at your home so that you will always return.

Rule of Three

Three is a favorite number of fairy tales. You get three wishes, three beds to choose from, and three wicked stepsisters. This love of three in tales comes from the trinity of the Father, Son, and Holy Spirit, and that trinity is really a copy of an older one: Maiden, Mother, and Crone. Three is a uniting number. The three card of the tarot, the Empress, shows a mother who is independent like a maiden but queenly and wise like a crone. You are strong, nurturing, and wise.

Number Seven and the Hermetic Principles

Seven is symbolic of intuition, philosophy, and reflection, which are all aspects of an alchemist. The Chariot is the seven card of the tarot and brings a quickness into a reading. It also depicts sphinxes in complete balance. In alchemy, there are seven principles that are attributed to Hermes or Thoth.

+ *Mentalism:* You create your own reality. Your thoughts are powerful, and you create with each and every one of them.

+ *Correspondence:* Every action has an effect, and this effect is infinite. The law of attraction is correspondence—energy is the basis of everything.

+ *Vibration:* Everything has a frequency, including you. Your vibration attracts like people, beings, and changes to you.

+ *Polarity:* Duality is an earthly reality. Opposites exist.

+ *Rhythm:* Energy is rhythmic; we see it in the moon, tides, hormones, and seasons.

+ *Cause and effect:* There is always a reaction to everything we think, feel, or do.

+ *Gender:* There is a divine feminine aspect and divine masculine aspect in each and every one of us, regardless of gender, and this is reflected all around us.

Sirius

Sirius was an important star in ancient Egypt, and the deities of Egypt may have been beings from Sirius. If you connect with the idea of being a starseed, then you have probably had a life not only in Egypt but on Sirius as well. Our Creator is as vast as the universe. Our souls are ancient and have incarnated in places other than earth. Being a starseed gives you a unique role on our planet at this time. More and more starseeds are incarnating to help shift the planet into a more enlightened age of being. Being a Sirius soul means that you have access to healing beyond earthly alchemy. Working with a moldavite crystal as an ally will open up your star memories and help awaken you more to your soul's purpose.

Egypt and Atlantis Connection

When heat is applied to a piece of amethyst, it alchemizes into what looks like citrine. Ancient Egypt is believed to be closely aligned with and inspired by Atlantis. Yes, you are an alchemist, but some of your healing will be found in the chapter on being a manifestor. Alchemy is used to manifest change. When you complete this chapter, go back to the one for citrine.

You are an alchemist. You are meant to transform yourself into gold. You are meant to shine with a light. You are connected to ancient Egypt, and working with the pantheon and the Egyptian *Book of the Dead* will serve you on this healing process. Learn some hieroglyphics and use them in your magical practice. Your sacred number of three is a reminder of the power of three. Say your incantations and prayers three times to strengthen them. Your number seven corresponds with the seven Hermetic or alchemical principles: mentalism, correspondence, vibration, polarity, rhythm, cause and effect, and gender. These principles are about duality and balance. You are above as well as below. You are what you think and create. You are both genders. You are the cause and the effect.

Notes on Amethyst

The following is a list that will help you go further on your path to becoming an alchemist. Use this list as a way to explore your archetype and create magic and rituals of your own.

- *Important past life:* ancient Egypt
- *Deities associated with this crystal:* Archangel Zadkiel, Isis, Osiris, Horus, all of the Egyptian pantheon, and Lion
- *Plant allies:* lavender, myrrh, oregano, ginger, and figs
- *Crystal and stone allies:* moldavite, emerald, labradorite, and all fluorites
- *Divination tool:* the tarot
- *Sacred numbers:* three and seven
- *Direction:* above
- *Element:* spirit/ether
- *Chakras:* crown and above

Chapter Ten
Working with the Crystals

As you continue to spend time with your Spirit Crystal, you will develop a stronger bond and strengthen your intuition. You will begin to devise your own spells, meditations, and rituals. You may get curious and begin to delve into the lessons of the other Spirit Crystals, realizing how to integrate their healing into your own journey. You should do this, as all the Spirit Crystals are sisters and brothers. They offer universal lessons for anyone on a spiritual path. The Spirit Crystals can also be combined for great works of magic, power, and healing. They are a soul family of crystalline beings and complement one another well. In this chapter, we will look at different ways to combine the crystals as well as how to develop a deeper relationship with your own Spirit Crystal by connecting with a crystal skull.

Using the Spirit Crystals as a Tool for Divination

A great way to get to know the Spirit Crystals is to use them for divination. You will need one of each Spirit Crystal. It is best if they are all a similar size and shape. The most optimal set would be small tumbled pieces. This practice works best if you have Spirit Crystals that are similar in shape and texture, meaning they are either all tumbled or all raw. Place the six crystals in a cloth bag or a box. Think of a question that is not yes or no and use the following descriptions to help you discern the answer. To divine, you can place the crystals in a natural fiber bag and shake the bag gently while you think of your query. Then take a deep breath and select a crystal from the bag. Alternatively, you can shake the crystals in your hand like you would to roll dice and let one drop for your answer. Over time, you will begin to know what the chosen crystal is communicating without using the book description.

+ *Clear quartz:* It is a time to think differently; get out of your head and find a new perspective. This crystal is symbolic of the energy of the Magician from the tarot. Pay attention to your health at this time. It could represent an astrological air sign or their time period on a calendar year: Gemini, Libra, or Aquarius. Consider the number four. It also represents communication: it is time to write, clear the air, or speak your truth.

+ *Rose quartz:* Rose quartz signifies the feminine energy and left side of the body. There is a connection to the Empress of the tarot. The answer is related to the heart. It is not one of logic and is instead one of grounded emotion. It could represent an earth sign or their time period on a calendar year: Taurus, Virgo, or Capricorn. Consider the number nine. It also represents love: self-love, romantic love, or parental love.

+ *Smoky quartz:* This crystal is the marker of death and rebirth. There is a connection to the Death card of the tarot. Smoky quartz characterizes a big change in energy. It could represent a water sign or their time period on a calendar year: Pisces, Cancer, or Scorpio. Consider the number eight. It is a time to ask: Is this ego, or is this truth? Discern what or whom to let go of. You are protected.

+ *Prasiolite:* It is a time to be in your own wisdom and instincts. What is your body already trying to tell you? There is a connection to the energy of the Fool from the tarot. It could represent a fire sign or their time period on a calendar year: Aries, Leo, or Sagittarius. Consider the number one. This crystal represents a time to slow down and not make quick decisions.

+ *Citrine:* Citrine signifies the masculine energy and right side of the body. This crystal is symbolic of the Chariot card of the tarot. It is a time to get grounded, put down roots, and dig your heels in. This can signify a time of incubation, a time to budget, or a time to plan or organize. Consider the number two. It is time to lead and allow yourself to be seen.

+ *Amethyst:* This crystal can signify a need for a vacation, gift, or taste of luxury. Think of the energy of the High Priestess of the tarot. There is a sense of fun and joy that's needed to be made a priority. Consider the numbers three and seven. This is a time to get out of your own head, play, do works of magic, seek beauty, and feel beautiful.

Making Crystal Grids

A crystal grid is an intentional arrangement of crystals created for a particular purpose. The purpose could be for spellwork, for ritual, or just to honor the crystals themselves. The grid can be arranged on an altar cloth, outside in the grass, around the home, or even on someone's body for healing. When combined into a grid, the Spirit Crystals offer even greater protection, power, and healing.

Crystal grids are used as a focused way to generate a source of power or healing using crystals and sacred geometry. Crystal gridding requires multiples of crystals. For the grids in this book, you will need multiples of the same crystals to make the designs, but you can combine the Spirit Crystals with their stone allies to create these grids. There is an infinite number of crystal grids to be created. The following are the grids that were given to me as a preference for each of the Spirit Crystals.

Sage's Wisdom: The Sage's Wisdom is a grid to connect you with your inner wisdom. It's a form of divination unique to gridding. The grid is a circle with four lines extending from the circle—sort of like a child's drawing of the sun. Once made, in the middle of the circle, you will place a question written on paper that has been concerning you. You can ask anything that you need an answer to. To make this grid, you begin with the question. As you place your crystals in a circle, concentrate on your question. Next, extend the circle into four lines outward. These lines represent the four directions and the possibilities of answers. Leave this grid in place until you have an answer come to you. In my experience, the answer usually comes the next day, so I recommend creating this grid before you go to sleep.

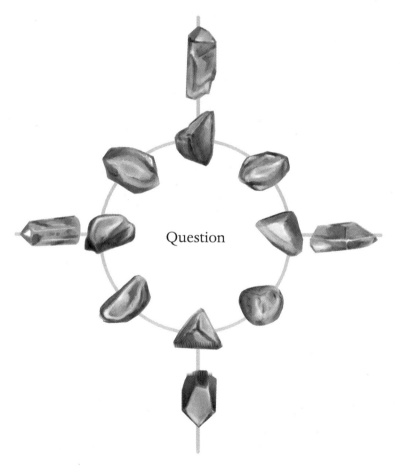

Sage's Wisdom

Medium's Cross: The Medium's Cross is used as a protection grid. You can make this grid anytime you feel you need extra protection spiritually, mentally, emotionally, or physically. To build this grid, you will create a cross that is of equal length, unlike the cross of Christianity. This cross represents harmony and the four elements. You can also use this grid in protective spells and rituals. It works great as a larger grid for your home as well. Find the southernmost point of your home and place a prasiolite crystal here. Then continue to place crystals in the other points in your home, putting smoky quartz in the west, rose quartz in the north, and clear quartz in the east.

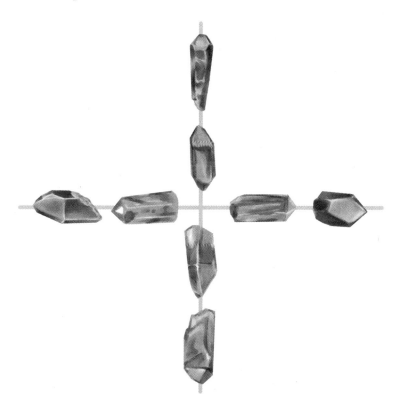

Medium's Cross

Avalon's Well: Avalon's Well is a grid for healing and love. The grid is an oval within an oval with a seashell, bowl of water, or a mirror in the center. The ovals symbolize eggs or seeds, which represent fertility. Fertility is not just for making babies. Fertility grids bring abundance to whatever aspect of our lives we need it. This could be healing, self-esteem, or love. We place a representation of water in the middle to give life to the fertility we are growing.

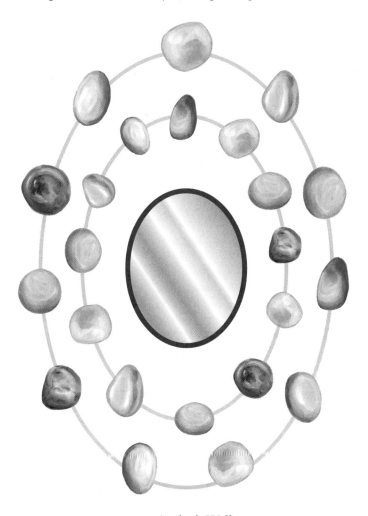

Avalon's Well

Lemurian Spiral: The spiral is an ancient, universal symbol. In Lemuria, the spiral was used to grid for manifesting or banishing. To create a manifesting spiral, begin by placing your first crystal on the outside of the spiral and grid inward. To make a banishing spiral, begin in the center and spiral your crystals outward. The spiral will work best with clear quartz. Try creating several spirals interlocking to make larger grids.

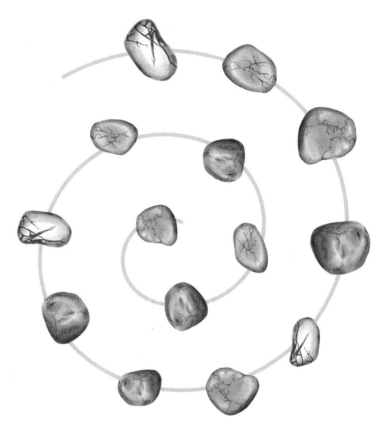

Lemurian Spiral

Atlantean Spiral: The Atlantean Spiral is not round like a traditional spiral. It is more like a pattern of alternating squares and diamonds. This grid is used to bring power. It can be created during a spell to add energy or used as a ritual itself. To lend this grid extra power, you can light a candle at its center. The fire energy adds to the magic of this grid.

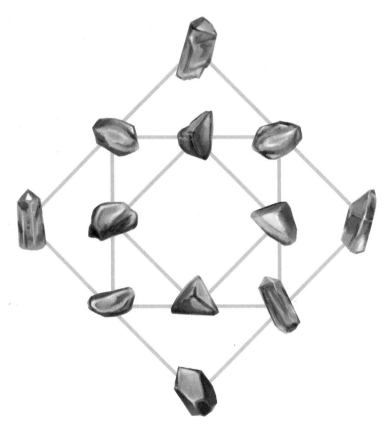

Atlantean Spiral

Alchemist's Pyramids: This Merkabah shape of two interlocking triangles represents the marriage of heaven and earth. The upward-facing triangle is earth and the downward-facing triangle is heaven, or the cosmos. The downward-facing pyramid or triangle also represents the divine feminine energy and the upward-facing triangle represents the masculine. This grid can be used to help create balance in your life. This grid can also be employed to create expansion as well as encourage deeper intuition.

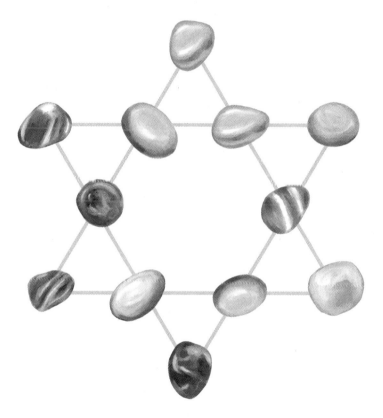

Alchemist's Pyramids

When creating a crystal grid, it's best to use your intuition and play with the shapes and the crystals you have. You can organize your crystals by color, shape, or type and then arrange them in a way that feels pleasing to you all with a particular purpose in mind. Making grids can be very meditative. You can also add herbs, shells, flowers, and charms to your grids. You can also play with the grid designs as well as the Spirit Crystals. For example, you could combine grids by making one of the grids larger with bigger pieces of crystal and then creating a miniature grid with chipped pieces of crystal in the center of the first grid.

RITUAL
Creating and Connecting to a Crystal Grid

Before you begin a grid, know the shape you want to create and have your crystals organized. Ready your mind. You may also want to ritualize this process by lighting a candle, burning incense, putting on high-vibrational music, or meditating beforehand. When you're ready, take a deep breath and close your eyes. Envision the shape you want to create with the crystals and focus on the reason you want to create the grid.

Open your eyes and touch each one of the crystals you have before you. Allow yourself to drop into this moment with the crystals. Then speak aloud your purpose for this grid. Speak to the crystals. Tell them why you need their energy. When you feel ready, create the grid.

Once you've made your grid, hold your hands over it and close your eyes. Take deep breaths until you feel a sense of ease. Then once again state the purpose of your grid and where you need this energy to go in your life. Thank the crystals, then open your eyes.

How long you leave a grid active is up to you. If you are consciously connecting with it daily, it can stay as is until you feel its purpose is served. If you are only connecting this one time and leaving it on an altar, then I would take it down after a moon cycle (new to full) has passed. Whenever you decide to undo, take apart, or open the grid, thank the crystals once again. Allow them to be cleansed and let them rest for at least a full day.

Combining the Magic of the Spirit Crystals

Each Spirit Crystal on its own is a healing tool, but when combined with another, their magic and purpose are altered to bring in new healing and medicine. Reference the following list when combining crystals to make a grid, ritual, or spell, or work on healing.

+ *Amethyst and rose quartz:* When combined, these two help you make a balanced decision between heart and mind. They help you with any issues surrounding justice. They help you wield your power in a loving way. They aid with boundary setting. When placed next to your bed, they help give prophetic dreams.

+ *Amethyst and smoky quartz:* These two crystals help connect to the realm of spirit. They combine for strong alchemy and transmutation. They create a sense of bravery. They help heal migraines and backaches.

+ *Amethyst and citrine:* When combined, amethyst and citrine help you in business creation and job-seeking. They aid in public speaking. They keep your mind clear. They are great for students and educators. Together, the two help with blood circulation.

+ *Amethyst and prasiolite:* Together these crystals give courage. They help foster independence. They help with all decision-making, especially when concerning moving. They are great for real estate decisions.

+ *Rose quartz and smoky quartz:* Used together, rose quartz and smoky quartz help open you to the forgiveness of others and yourself. They help release anxiety and give a sense of calm. Placed by a front door they keep away the negative and draw in the positive. Kept together in your car they help with safe and peaceful traveling.

+ *Rose quartz and citrine:* Together these crystals help balance the divine feminine and masculine within your body and being. They help with self-expression, especially in a business setting. They help heal emotional wounds. When put together in a home, they bring harmony, peace, and abundance.

+ *Rose quartz and prasiolite:* Together they heal any issues concerning self-esteem, especially with body image. They help connect you to your inner Buddha or highest self. They help give a sense of calm and peace, allowing you to be yourself fully.

+ *Smoky quartz and citrine:* When combined in a place of business, smoky quartz and citrine keep money or abundance in and debt out. They help you manifest and turn dreams into reality. They help with organization and are great to keep around while making lists, doing taxes, or filling out a résumé.

+ *Smoky quartz and prasiolite:* Together they help lift depression. They aid in meditation and help to calm "the monkey mind." Place them in living rooms or other common meeting areas for a lighter and more harmonious atmosphere.

+ *Citrine and prasiolite:* Combined these crystals help you thrive in a leadership position. They aid in making wise money choices and are good to have near when working on your budget. Keep tiny pieces in your purse, wallet, or piggy bank.

+ *Clear quartz:* Clear quartz amplifies any of the other Spirit Crystals and can be used to add clarity and power to any of the other combinations. It can also help to stabilize and cleanse the other crystals while they "work." I always place at least one clear quartz in every grid I make.

The magical combinations of the Spirit Crystals are not limited to what is listed here. You will find new ways and meanings as you get to know the Spirit Crystals and work with them. They can be combined for meditation practices, grids, spells, and other reasons you discover. Allow yourself to play and create with the Spirit Crystals.

Crystal Skulls

A crystal is connected to a collective soul, and most tumbling and shaping doesn't change its inherent magic. However, when a quartz crystal is shaped into a skull, both its power and its potential for healing are altered. It becomes even more of a conduit and a teacher than just a healer. A crystal skull can wake up with the same activation process taught earlier in the book; however, a crystal skull will likely give a name, as each one houses a Spirit Guide or Guardian connected to its shape and type of crystal. Some crystal skulls can be purchased fully awake with a name, and others must be awoken by you.

Δ Brief History of Crystal Skulls

The original crystal skulls are a gift from the thirteen original clan mothers. The clan mothers came earthside to teach humanity various lessons. When each mother's soul returned to the Creator, a pure human-sized crystal skull was left behind. According to Indigenous author Jamie Sams, "each one of the Crystal Skulls was housed in a place where women gather to share Medicine."[2] These sacred sites were scattered throughout modern North and South America. This includes the ocean islands (Lemuria and Atlantis). Each one of these skulls was encoded with all the wisdom of the earth. They are the record keepers.

According to Leon, a Navajo elder interviewed by Chris Morton and Ceri Louise Thomas, the crystal skulls make a map on the earth and are to remain where they are to help humanity and the earth evolve. He, like Jamie Sams, explains that these skulls were crafted by the Creator for the purpose of storing all the wisdom, much like libraries. He also explains that the skulls vibrate at a certain frequency that all of us can feel. The vibration is like a calling, and it is why many of us are drawn to crystal skulls. He says that we can connect to this tone and realize the true sound of creation. "The wisdom of the skulls becomes available when you open yourself to this mystery and let the sound come in."[3] This is the purpose of working with a crystal skull—to take you to deeper levels of awareness and healing.

One such skull might have been found in an archaeological site at Lubaantun in the 1920s. Known as the skull of doom, or the Mitchel-Hedges skull, this skull has had the most research conducted on it and has been widely written

---

2. Sams, *The 13 Original Clan Mothers*, 303.
3. Morton and Thomas, *The Mystery of the Crystal Skulls*, 252.

about. The story is that it was discovered by a seventeen-year-old girl named Anna. Anna's stepfather was like a real-life Indiana Jones, and while visiting an archaeological site in Belize, she could see the glint of the skull. It was she who was lowered down to retrieve it. This skull's original location was in a place where the Mayans thrived, which lines up perfectly with the knowledge shared by Jamie Sams and the connection to the clan mothers. According to Carole Davis, who connected with the skull, the Mitchell-Hedges skull was from Atlantis and encoded with Atlantean knowledge and wisdom.[4]

Modern-day crystal skulls are all fashioned after and connected with the original thirteen skulls. When you purchase a crystal skull and connect to it, you are proclaiming that you are open to reclaiming wisdom, connecting with a Spirit Guide, and wanting to dive into the records of the earth and beyond. I say beyond because I know that some of the crystals have been encoded by starbeings or Sky People to hold the wisdom of their star systems and dying planets as well. When you purchase a traveler or starbeing skull, you are opening to a galactic guide and opening to galactic records.

Journal Pause

- How do you feel about working with a skull?
- What kinds of skull(s) are you drawn to and why?

Choosing a Skull

When choosing a skull, all the previous advice on crystal shopping is relevant. You can purchase them online, and if you do, look for descriptions of being hand carved and, even better, look for a carver's name attributed. There are actually rehoming groups and web pages where you can purchase skulls that are already activated and usually well taken care of.

---

4. Bowen, Nocerino, and Shapiro, *Mysteries of the Crystal Skulls Revealed*, 256.

Types of Skulls

There are different styles of skulls to choose from, and the type of guidance that comes through varies based on style, so let your heart lead you to the guide you need.

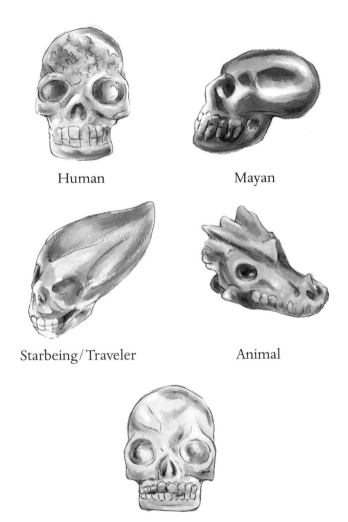

Human

Mayan

Starbeing/Traveler

Animal

Magical Child

Skull Types

- *Human:* From tiny to life-size to beyond life-size, human crystal skulls tend to be the easiest skulls to find and will often connect you to past lives here on earth. Two of my skulls are Lemurian quartz, and both are guides from Lemuria. So again, the shape and material are important to consider.

- *Mayan:* Mayan skulls are humanlike with an elongated crown. They are powerful for anyone but especially those connected to smoky quartz. The guides tend to be Mayan or of starbeing origin.

- *Starbeing/traveler:* These alien skulls connect you to galactic guides, so if you feel you are a starseed, meaning your soul has spent at least one incarnation on another planet, this type of skull may help you heal and connect to that life.

- *Animal:* Animal skulls are rarer, and the most common is the dragon. Dragons are amazing. They help burn away lower karma and are fiercely protective guides. A dragon skull would be ideal for someone with a past life in Atlantis.

- *Magical child:* The magical child skull looks humanoid with a bigger crown. Since we are shifting into 5D or new earth energy, working with this kind of skull will accelerate the healing.

RITUAL
Connecting to a Skull

Once you have chosen a skull, if it has not already been activated, you will want to follow the cleansing and activation steps you learned previously. At the end of the activation, invite a being of highest consciousness to use the skull to communicate with you. If you sense one already present, invite them to wake up. If you are more audient, open your eyes and look into the eyes of the skull and ask for a name. If you are more visual, you can press your fingers lightly into the eye sockets and with eyes closed ask for a name. If you prefer automatic writing to channel or receive information, hold the skull in your nondominant hand, look into its eyes, and allow your hand to be guided. A name may come that you aren't sure how to spell or pronounce, or you may see it in your mind's eye as a symbol. If you need clarification, just ask your skull again.

If you don't receive anything the first time, try cleansing and activating again. If after two times you don't feel a connection or receive a name, cleanse your skull and give it time in the sunlight. Sometimes a skull will need time to heal from whatever trauma it endured before it reached you. Once you have established a connection, continue to meditate with your skull. You can also go back to your Spirit Place, which you have established previously, and invite the Spirit Guide of the skull to meet you there. This will help you see them in another form and build a deeper bond.

How to Care for Your Skull

Crystal skulls want to be with you. Don't put them in pouches or drawers. I have a tiny one that I sometimes carry with me, and I make sure to give it lots of time out of the darkness after doing so. They like sunshine and moonlight. They like to be near other skulls, so if you start collecting them, you may find they like to be clustered or gridded together. In general, I don't let other people touch them. I also periodically cleanse them when they seem like they need it. Once you connect with the skull, you will know intuitively when they need a cleanse.

Working with a Skull

A crystal skull made of your Spirit Crystal will accelerate your healing process. As you heal, you step deeper into the power of your archetype. The skull guide can be called on to help in any meditation, spell, or ritual. Here are some ideas of how to work specifically with your skull once they are activated and their name is known.

RITUAL
Journalling for Answers

Your skull houses a guide, and you can bring them questions you would like answered. These questions can be about the past, the present, or the future. For this exercise, come up with some deeper questions you would like answered. Write these questions down, leaving spaces for answers. If you don't have any particular questions, you can write, "What do you want me to know at this time?" Leave these questions overnight with your skull, wherever it rests.

The next day, sit in meditation with your skull and ask for the answers. Depending on how you receive channeled information, you might receive the answer through automatic writing, see it as a picture, or even hear it. The more you practice this kind of communication with your skull, the stronger the bond will be and the faster the answers will arrive. They may even arrive in your dreams at night. Your skull makes a great divination partner. Whether you read cards or runes or work with a pendulum, have your skull near you to help you see further and with clarity.

RITUAL
Clearing Your Head

Since your crystal skull is a head, it can be used in sympathetic magic. If you are having trouble making a decision, seeing an answer, or coming up with an idea, perform this ritual. It can even be done if you're just feeling foggy. Cast a protective circle, light a white candle, and hold your skull to your heart. Take deep breaths to settle yourself.

Place your skull on your forehead so that you are connected third eye to third eye, then say, "(Skull's name), thank you for clearing my mind, opening my third eye, and helping me see what I haven't seen." Slowly pull the skull from your third eye and visualize or feel a thread of light connecting your third eye to the third eye of your skull. Then rub the third eye of your skull. Rub it in upward motions with your fingers.

Look into the third eye area of your skull and visualize a fog lifting, a cloud passing, or a door opening. Then say, "I see clearly now. And so it is." When you are ready, visualize the thread of light dissolving and close your circle. You should now feel more clearheaded and balanced.

SPELL
Sending Your Skull on a Mission

Your skull houses a particular kind of guide. They came to you at this time for a reason. You can sit in meditation and ask what they are here to help you with, or you may have a sense of it already. I have one skull who is here to help with my career, another who likes to travel with me, another who helps me give Reiki and read cards, and others that watch over my children (yes, they are safe and great for kids). Once you understand your skull guide's mission, you can begin to ask them to help you with different jobs or tasks. Here is a list of jobs that are great for a skull guide, but know that you are not limited to these ideas.

+ *Dreamwork:* A skull guide can keep you protected in the dreamtime. Keep them by your bed and ask them for protection and guidance as you work in your sleep.

+ *Manifesting:* Communicate the changes you desire to your skull guide, then create an altar that represents these changes. Place your skull in the center and ask them to help guide this change in your life. Talk to them daily about this, and don't keep them on the altar for more than a full lunar cycle.

+ *Protection:* Ask your skull guide to protect you, a loved one, or a home. Ask them to watch over you or your home and face them toward a front door, place them in a bedroom facing the bed, or keep them with you. They are extremely protective and will give you a stronger sense of intuition.

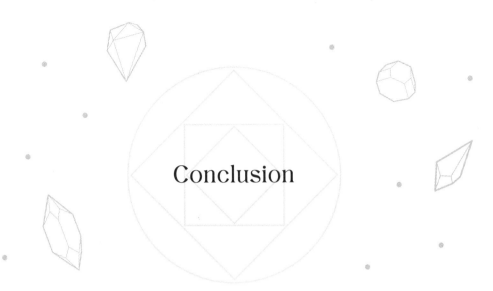

Conclusion

The Spirit Crystals are here to help shift your soul into a place of healed wholeness. They are allies on this journey toward embodying your archetype. Spirit Crystals are enlightened and have come from Mother Earth and beyond to share their gifts with us. They are special, and working with one is a lifelong process. You now have a companion to help heal and guide you, one to open doors to heal your past and manifest a better future. Honor yourself and your crystals in your work. Allow yourself to come home again. Allow yourself to be at peace.

Crystals are sentient. The more you connect with them and listen to them, the more you will know their aliveness. To dig deeper on this journey, allow yourself the time and space to connect with your Spirit Crystal. In modern times, so many crystals are available. But what if you don't need all the crystals but just a few of the same crystals? This is a question I hope was answered for you. I am by no means a minimalist, but simplicity in spirituality is a luxury. When we first go down a spiritual path, many of us wander and try many things. We collect books, decks, charms, crystals, herbs, and other items we hope will offer us healing and guide our evolution.

There is a real beauty in this spiritual chaos. It's exhilarating to try it all. It's exciting to be led on different paths. But if all we do is continue going to the next thing or the next crystal, how can we really understand the healing of what we have already? Crystals move slowly. Stones evolve and change in the rock cycle over hundreds—sometimes millions—of years. It's impossible to get to know such an ancient and slow-moving being in days. The lessons the Spirit Crystals have for us are for lifetimes. It's time to slow down, connect, and listen. Allow yourself the luxury of simplicity and not searching for the next thing yet. Instead, develop a true relationship and understanding of your Spirit Crystal.

Acknowledgments

Thank you to my husband, Ben, and children, Lucy and Zach, for all the love and support. I cannot express how much your support means to me. You three have been my biggest cheerleaders on my road to becoming an author. I appreciate every time you have stopped and looked for rocks with me for hours and hours without complaint.

Thank you to my family and friend support team! Shout-out to Aunt Amber, Jessie, Mayra, and many more. Thank you all for cheering me on and celebrating my wins.

Thank you to Lynnette for being an amazing advocate and literary agent.

Thank you to Llewellyn and each person who helped make this book a reality. I cannot express how exciting it is for me to call myself a Llewellyn author.

Thank you to Our Coven for all the love, support, and fun!

Thank you to the Spirit Crystals, crystal skulls, and Stone People of my home, land, and earth.

Resources

For more on crystals:

Any book by Judy Hall makes a wonderful resource, specifically her Crystal Bible series, which has three volumes. She also wrote *Crystal Skulls: Ancient Tools for Peace, Knowledge, and Enlightenment,* which is a deep dive into the world of crystal skulls. These are great books for anyone looking to work with and understand a large variety of crystals and stones.

For more on herbs:

Henriette's Herbal (https://www.henriettes-herb.com/index.html) is an organized, in-depth look at many herbs and classic information about them.

Herbalista (https://herbalista.org/) has a wealth of herbal information. The site's mission is to spread herbal information to everyone, and it is a great resource to look for recipes and classes.

For more on ancient societies:

Lemuria & Atlantis: Studying the Past to Survive the Future by Shirley Andrews is an interesting read. It's one of the few books written on these places. The fictional work *The Mists of Avalon* by Marion Zimmer Bradley is a great read for anyone who feels a calling to Avalon.

For more on Indigenous practices and creation stories:

Jamie Sams left a legacy behind including card decks and books with deep wisdom she collected from elders as well as her own experience. She writes about the crystal skulls, Lemuria, starbeings, and Stone People. I recommend beginning with *The 13 Original Clan Mothers: The Sacred Path to Discovering the Gifts, Talents, and Abilities of the Feminine Through Ancient Teachings of the Sisterhood.* Alberto Villoldo, PhD, also has quite the wealth of wisdom and knowledge spread throughout his many books and card decks. *The Four Insights: Wisdom, Power, and Grace of the Earthkeepers* is a great book to start with. Both Sams and Villoldo are the best resources I have found on working with animal guides as well.

For more on mindfulness and meditation:

Thich Nhat Hanh was a truly special human being and author. Any of his books will help you understand yourself and your own mind. Plum Village (https://plumvillage.org/) has a wealth of information as well as an app you can use to learn meditation for free.

For more on chakras:

Chakras: Energy Centers of Transformation by Harish Johari is my favorite book I have read on the subject. It also has helpful illustrations and an opportunity to color.

For more on angels and ascended masters:

Kyle Gray is the Angel Whisperer for a reason. His books, card decks, and classes are easy to understand and full of useful information. He has taken a lot of what spiritualism left behind and modernized it.

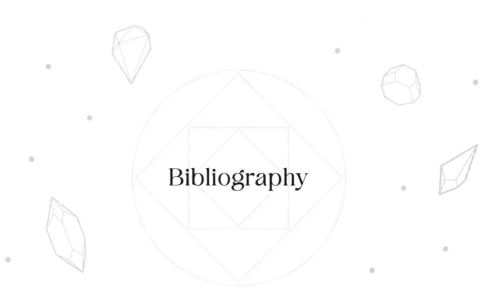

Bibliography

Alvarado, Denise. *The Marie Laveau Voodoo Grimoire: Rituals, Recipes, and Spells for Healing, Protection, Beauty, Love, and More*. Weiser Books, 2024.

Andrews, Shirley. *Lemuria and Atlantis: Studying the Past to Survive the Future*. Llewellyn Publications, 2004.

Bell, Jenny. "Crystals: Using Intuition to Heal, Make Grids and Work Professionally with Certification." Udemy. 2 hours, 26 min. https://www.udemy.com/course/crystals-using-intuition/.

Bell, Jenny. "Finding Your Spirit Crystal: Become a Certified Guide." Udemy. 2 hours, 35 min. https://www.udemy.com/course/draft/4549560/.

Bowen, Sandra, F. R. "Nick" Nocerino, and Joshua Shapiro. *Mysteries of the Crystal Skull Revealed*. J & S Aquarian Networking, 1988.

Campbell, Joseph. *Pathways to Bliss: Mythology and Personal Transformation*. New World Library, 2004.

Cunningham, Scott. *Cunningham's Encyclopedia of Magical Herbs*. Llewellyn Publications, 2007.

Cunningham, Scott. *Wicca: A Guide for the Solitary Practitioner*. Llewellyn Publications, 1997.

Dolfyn. *Crystal and Gemstone Directory*. Vol. 6 of *Crystal Wisdom*. Earthspirit, 1988.

Dolfyn. *Crystal Wisdom: Spiritual Properties of Crystals and Gemstones*. Earthspirit, 1989.

The Editors of Encyclopaedia Britannica. "Medium." Last updated August 25, 2023. https://www.britannica.com/topic/medium-occultism /additional-info#history.

Feldman, David B. "The Power of Journaling." *Psychology Today*. September 20, 2020. https://www.psychologytoday.com/us/blog/supersurvivors/202009 /the-power-journaling.

"Four Crystals and Crystallization." Open Geology. Accessed February 26, 2024. https://opengeology.org/Mineralogy/4-crystals-and-crystallization/.

Gray, Kyle. *Angel Prayers: Harnessing the Help of Heaven to Create Miracles*. Hay House, 2018.

Gray, Kyle. "Crystal Skull Workshop." Presentation. May 2, 2021.

Gray, Kyle. *Divine Masters, Ancient Wisdom: Activations to Connect with Universal Spirit Guides*. Hay House, 2021.

Greenacre, David. *Numerology and You*. Lancer Books, 1971.

Gold, Gari. *Crystal Energy: Put the Power in the Palm of Your Hand*. Contemporary Books, 1987.

Hall, Judy. *The Crystal Bible: A Definitive Guide to Crystals*. Octopus Publishing Group, 2009.

Hall, Judy. *Crystal Skulls: Ancient Tools for Peace, Knowledge, and Enlightenment*. Weiser Books, 2016.

Hanh, Thich Nhat. "The Four Layers of Consciousness." Lion's Road. Accessed August 27, 2023. https://www.lionsroar.com/the-four-layers -of-consciousness/.

Harlow, S. M. *A Tea Witch's Grimoire: Magickal Recipes for Your Teatime*. Weiser Books, 2023.

Hart, Francene. *Sacred Geometry Oracle Deck*. Bear, 2001.

Hoeller, Stephan A. *The Royal Road: A Manual of Kabalistic Meditations on the Tarot*. Theosophical Publishing House, 1980.

Howe, Linda. *How to Read the Akashic Records: Accessing the Archive of the Soul and Its Journey*. Sounds True, 2009.

Hughes, Aimee. "The Meaning of Om Mani Padme Hum." Yogapedia. Updated February 19, 2020. https://www.yogapedia.com/2/8623/meditation /mantra/the-meaning-of-om-mani-padme-hum.

Johari, Harish. *Chakras: Energy Centers of Transformation.* Destiny Books, 1987.

Marashinsky, Amy Sophia. *The Goddess Oracle Deck.* Illustrated by Hrana Janto. U. S. Games, 2006.

Mauney-Brodek, Lorna. "Courses." Herbalista Free School. Accessed January 14, 2025. https://herbalista.teachable.com/courses/.

"Mohs Hardness Scale." National Park Service. Updated April 12, 2023. https:// www.nps.gov/articles/mohs-hardness-scale.htm.

Monaghan, Patricia. *The Goddess Path: Myths, Invocations & Rituals.* Llewellyn Publications, 2000.

Morton, Chris, and Ceri Louise Thomas. *The Mystery of the Crystal Skulls: A Real Life Detective Story of the Ancient World.* Bear, 1998.

"Om Tara Tu Tara Tu Ray Swaha." Yogapedia. Updated December 21, 2023. https://www.yogapedia.com/definition/10865/om-tara-tu-tara-tu-ray -swaha.

Sams, Jamie. *Sacred Path Cards: The Discovery of Self Through Native Teachings.* HarperSanFrancisco, 1990.

Sams, Jamie. *The 13 Original Clan Mothers: Your Sacred Path to Discovering the Gifts, Talents, and Abilities of the Feminine Through Ancient Teachings of the Sisterhood.* HarperSanFrancisco, 1993.

Sesay, Adama. *Black Moon Lilith Rising: How to Unlock the Power of the Dark Divine Feminine through Astrology.* Hay House, 2023.

"Shambhala – The Birth Place of Kalki, the Final Incarnation of Vishnu." Sanskriti Magazine. Accessed August 25, 2023. https://www .sanskritimagazine.com/shambhala-birth-place-kalki-final-incarnation -vishnu/.

Tello, Julio C. "Finding El Dorado: The Search for the Treasure of Paititi." Karikuy Tours, November 30, 2009. https://www.karikuy .com/finding-el-dorado-the-search-for-el-gran-paititi/.

Villoldo, Alberto. *The Four Insights: Wisdom, Power, and Grace of the Earthkeepers.* Hay House, 2006.

Villoldo, Alberto. "The Power Animals Online Course." The Four Winds Society. June 2023.

Villoldo, Alberto. *Shaman, Healer, Sage: How to Heal Yourself and Others with the Energy Medicine of the Americas.* Harmony Books, 2000.

Walker, Dael. *The Crystal Book.* Crystal, 1984.

Index

A

C

D

E

G

T